Against the 5AM Myth

Thriving as a Night Owl

Why Success Doesn't Start at 5AM—and How to Build a Life That Fits Your Rhythm

Wilson Emmanuel Brown

First Edition

ISBN: 978-1-923604-56-8

The information contained in this book is for general informational and educational purposes only. It is not intended as a substitute for professional medical, psychological, or sleep disorder treatment. The author and publisher make no representations or warranties of any kind with respect to the accuracy or completeness of the contents of this book.

While the strategies and techniques described in this book are based on scientific research and have been used successfully by many individuals, results may vary. The author and publisher shall not be liable for any loss of profit or any other commercial damages, including but not limited to special, incidental, consequential, or other damages.

Readers are advised to consult with qualified healthcare professionals before making significant changes to their sleep schedules, especially if they have existing medical conditions, sleep disorders, or take medications that may be affected by schedule changes.

The names and identifying details of individuals mentioned in case studies and examples have been changed to protect privacy. Any resemblance to actual persons, living or dead, or actual events is purely coincidental.

The author and publisher disclaim any responsibility for adverse effects or consequences resulting from the use of any suggestions, preparations, or procedures described in this book. Readers should use their own judgment and consult healthcare professionals regarding their specific circumstances.

Table of Contents

Preface

The 4:30 AM Alarm That Changed Everything

It was 4:30 AM on a Tuesday morning in February when I finally admitted defeat.

The alarm had been going off at this ungodly hour for three months straight. Three months of forcing myself out of bed in the darkness, stumbling through a "miracle morning routine" that was supposed to transform my life. Three months of meditation that felt like torture, journaling that produced nothing but complaints about being tired, and workouts that left me more exhausted than energized.

I was following the advice of every productivity guru, success coach, and self-help book on the market. I had bought into the promise that waking up at 5 AM—or better yet, 4:30 AM—was the secret to unlocking my potential. After all, successful people wake up early. The early bird gets the worm. If I wanted to join the ranks of high achievers, I needed to start my day before the sun came up.

But as I sat on the edge of my bed that February morning, too tired to think straight, I realized something profound: This wasn't working. Not only was I not becoming more successful, I was becoming more miserable. I was chronically exhausted, irritable with everyone around me, and producing some of the worst work of my career. The "golden hours" of the morning felt more like fool's gold—shiny on the surface but worthless in reality.

That morning, I did something that felt revolutionary: I turned off the alarm and went back to sleep.

When I woke up naturally at 9 AM, something extraordinary happened. For the first time in months, my mind felt clear. My energy was stable. I actually wanted to start my day. By 10 PM that evening, I had accomplished more meaningful work than I had in weeks of forced early mornings.

It was the beginning of a journey that would completely transform how I understood productivity, success, and human biology.

The Personal Cost of Fighting Your Nature

Like many night owls, I had spent years believing there was something wrong with me. In college, while my roommates were bright-eyed at 8 AM lectures, I was struggling to keep my eyes open. In my first corporate job, I watched colleagues bound into morning meetings with enthusiasm while I nursed my third cup of coffee and tried to form coherent thoughts.

I told myself I was lazy. Undisciplined. Lacking willpower.

The shame was overwhelming. I tried everything: going to bed earlier (which just meant lying awake staring at the ceiling), light therapy, melatonin supplements, cold showers, accountability partners. I read every morning routine book, listened to countless productivity podcasts, and followed the advice of internet gurus who promised that early rising was the key to everything I wanted in life.

Nothing worked sustainably. I would force myself into an early schedule for a few weeks or months, only to crash back into my natural rhythm, feeling like a failure each time.

What I didn't understand then—what no one was talking about—was that I wasn't broken. I was simply fighting my biology.

The Science That Set Me Free

The turning point came when I discovered the research on chronotypes—our individual biological tendencies toward being morning larks or night owls. I learned that approximately 40-60% of the population naturally leans toward eveningness, and that this preference is largely genetic, not a character flaw.

I discovered that my brain literally wasn't designed to function optimally at 6 AM. When I forced myself to wake up early, I was asking my prefrontal cortex—the part responsible for complex thinking and decision-making—to perform while still marinated in melatonin, the sleep hormone.

It would be like asking a marathon runner to compete while wearing ankle weights and then criticizing them for running slowly.

The research revealed that night owls aren't just different from morning larks—in many ways, we're advantaged. Evening types tend to exhibit higher levels of creativity, perform better on tasks requiring complex problem-solving, and show greater cognitive flexibility. We have sustained attention and energy when others are winding down.

But here's the kicker: our culture has been designed around the preferences of morning larks. The 9-to-5 schedule, the emphasis on early rising, the assumption that productivity happens before noon—all of this is biased toward about 25% of the population while ignoring the needs of everyone else.

Why I wrote this book

This book was written because I refused to accept that half the population should suffer in silence.

After years of research, experimentation, and working with hundreds of fellow night owls, I've developed what I call the Anti-5AM approach—a complete paradigm shift that honors your biology instead of fighting it.

This isn't about sleeping until noon or being unproductive. It's about recognizing that peak performance looks different for different people. It's about building routines and systems that work with your natural energy patterns instead of against them.

It's about understanding that when you wake up doesn't determine your worth, your work ethic, or your potential for success.

Who This Book Is For?

This book is for every person who has ever felt guilty about hitting the snooze button.

It's for the creative professionals who do their best work at 11 PM but are told they should be "morning people."

It's for the corporate employees who survive morning meetings on caffeine and willpower while waiting for their brain to boot up.

It's for the entrepreneurs who've been told that successful business owners wake up at 5 AM, even though their most innovative ideas come to them after sunset.

It's for the parents who feel like failures because they can't be cheerful and energetic at 6 AM, not realizing that being present and attentive in the evening is just as valuable.

It's for anyone who has ever wondered if there's something wrong with them because the "miracle morning" feels more like punishment than transformation.

If you've ever felt like you're swimming upstream in a world designed for early birds, this book is for you.

What You'll Find Here

This isn't another productivity book that assumes everyone's brain works the same way. Instead, you'll find:

Science-backed strategies that honor your chronotype rather than fighting it.

Flexible frameworks instead of rigid schedules, because real life doesn't follow a perfect routine.

Practical solutions for thriving in a 9-to-5 world when your biology says otherwise.

Permission to stop apologizing for your natural rhythm and start leveraging it as a competitive advantage.

You'll learn how to create mornings that energize rather than exhaust you, how to manage your energy instead of just your time, and how to build a life that works with your biology instead of against it.

A Movement, Not Just a Method

The Anti-5AM isn't just about changing your morning routine—it's about changing how we think about productivity, success, and human potential.

It's about recognizing that diversity in chronotypes is a feature, not a bug. In our hunter-gatherer ancestors, having both early risers and night owls in the group provided survival advantages—someone was always alert and keeping watch.

Today, in our knowledge-based economy, we need that same diversity. We need the deep thinkers who hit their stride in the evening. We need the creative problem-solvers who find clarity in the quiet hours after sunset. We need the sustained focus that comes naturally to evening types when others are winding down.

Your most productive, creative, and fulfilling life is waiting for you. It's just not waiting at 5 AM.

P.S. — If you're reading this book at 11 PM while everyone else is asleep, you're in good company. Some of us do our best thinking when the world is quiet and the distractions have faded. That's not a bug—it's a feature.

Wilson Emmanuel Brown

The Tyranny of the Alarm Clock

You know the sound.

It's that jarring noise that rips you out of sleep when the world is still dark. It doesn't matter if it's a gentle chime or a blaring alarm; it feels like an accusation. You fumble for the snooze button, your head heavy, your eyes stinging.

You buy yourself nine more minutes. But those minutes aren't restful. They are filled with anxiety and guilt. You start running through the list of things you *should* be doing. You *should* be meditating, or exercising, or getting a head start on work. The successful people on the internet are already three hours into their day.

When you finally drag yourself out of bed, you don't feel energized. You feel defeated. You're already behind.

If this sounds familiar, you've been living under the tyranny of the alarm clock. You've been trying to force yourself into a mold that doesn't fit. And you've probably been blaming yourself, telling yourself that your inability to wake up early is a personal failure.

This book is here to tell you something you need to hear: The problem isn't you. The problem is the irrational advice you've been trying to follow.

The Misery of the Forced Morning

Let's look at what it really feels like to force yourself awake when your body isn't ready. It's not just being "a little sleepy." It's a physical slog.

Your brain feels foggy. Simple tasks, like making coffee or finding your keys, feel complicated. You might feel irritable, clumsy, or even slightly nauseous. This state is sometimes called *sleep inertia*. It's the feeling that your brain is still trying to boot up, like an old computer struggling to load its operating system.

For some people, this fog lifts in 15 minutes. If you're reading this book, it likely lasts much longer for you—maybe an hour, maybe three.

Now, let's add the emotional weight. When you struggle through this fog, what are you telling yourself?

- "I'm so lazy."
- "Why can't I just get it together?"
- "I'll never be successful if I can't even wake up on time."

These beliefs are painful. And frankly, they are nonsense. You are demanding that your body behave in a way it is not built to behave. And when it naturally resists, you beat yourself up.

We spend a lot of time "awfulizing" our sleep patterns. We turn a simple preference for later mornings into a catastrophe, convinced it means we are failing at life.

Consider the experience of a graphic designer who spent years trying to adapt. This person believed that to be truly professional, they *must* be at their desk by 7:00 AM. They forced it, but the mornings were agonizing. They produced their worst work during those early hours, staring blankly at the screen, moving pixels around without any real creativity. The guilt was immense. They thought, "If I were more disciplined, this would work." But by 9:00 PM, when they were supposed to be winding down, their creativity sparked. They would often work until midnight, producing brilliant designs, only to feel exhausted and guilty the next morning when the cycle repeated.

The misery didn't come from the schedule itself; it came from the belief that they absolutely *must* follow that schedule to be worthwhile. It's time to challenge that belief.

The 5AM Lie

Where did this obsession with early rising come from?

Over the past decade, a powerful narrative has taken hold. It's often called Hustle Culture. It suggests that every minute you are not working, optimizing, or improving yourself is a minute wasted.

At the center of this culture is the "5AM " concept. The idea is simple and seductive: Wake up at 5 AM and use that "golden hour" for intense self-improvement before the rest of the world logs on. Books, podcasts, and social media influencers push this relentlessly. They show images of dark, quiet streets, sweaty post-workout selfies, and checklists completed by 7 AM.

It looks great on social media. It sells millions of books. But there's a fundamental flaw in the logic.

The 5AM Lie is the belief that *one specific routine* is the universal key to success for *all people*.

This is simply not true. It ignores basic human variation. It's like telling everyone in the world they must wear a size 9 shoe. If your feet are a size 11, a size 9 shoe isn't a "challenge to overcome"; it's just a bad fit. It will cause pain, blisters, and make it harder to walk.

The advice to wake up at 5 AM is a bad fit for approximately 40 to 60 percent of the population. That's nearly half of us.

When the dominant culture tells you that you must do something you are biologically unsuited for, and you fail, you feel excluded. You see the "early birds" celebrated, while you are labeled as disorganized, sluggish, or unmotivated.

The 5AM Lie thrives on a few irrational beliefs that we need to confront:

1. **The Moralization of Sleep:** This is the notion that waking up early is inherently virtuous, while sleeping later is lazy or indulgent. Let's be clear: When you wake up has no bearing on your moral worth.
2. **The Belief in Scarcity:** The idea that there are only a few "good" hours in the day (usually the early ones), and if you miss them, you've lost your chance. This ignores the fact that high-quality work can happen at any time.
3. **The One-Size-Fits-All Fallacy:** The assumption that everyone's biology works the same way and that discipline can overcome genetics.

We have attached a moral value to the time we wake up. Early is good. Late is bad. This book is about breaking that connection. Success is not about when you start; it's about what you accomplish and how you feel while doing it.

You Aren't Lazy

If you struggle to wake up early and feel more alert and creative in the evening, there is a word for what you are. You are a *night owl*.

This is not a habit. It's not a character flaw. It's biology.

Let's dismantle the most damaging myth first: The idea that if you struggle with mornings, you are lazy. This is false.

Scientists who study sleep patterns refer to this as your *chronotype*. Your chronotype is your body's natural tendency to sleep and wake at certain times. It's largely genetic. It's baked into your DNA just as much as your height or your eye color.

Roughly speaking, people fall into three categories:

1. **Larks (Morning Types):** These are the 5 AM people. They naturally wake up early, feel most energized in the morning, and wind down early in the evening.
2. **Owls (Evening Types):** They struggle to wake up early. Their energy levels peak in the afternoon or evening. They find it difficult to fall asleep early.
3. **Hummingbirds (Intermediate Types):** They fall somewhere in the middle, usually following a more traditional schedule.

The world, especially the traditional corporate world, is built for Larks. The 9-to-5 schedule forces Owls to start their day during their biological low point.

If you are a night owl, your internal clock is simply set later. Your body doesn't start producing melatonin (the sleep hormone) until later in the evening. And it doesn't stop producing it until later in the morning.

This means that when a night owl tries to wake up at 5 AM, their body is still in full sleep mode. It's biologically equivalent to an early bird trying to wake up at 2 AM. You wouldn't expect an early bird to be productive at 2 AM. So why do we expect night owls to be productive at 5 AM?

When you accept your wiring, things start to change. You stop asking, "What's wrong with me?" and start asking, "How can I make my schedule work for me?"

Recognizing your biology is the first step to optimizing your life. You cannot shame yourself into becoming a morning person.

My Promise to you

This book will not try to turn you into a morning person. If you are a night owl, you will likely always be a night owl. And that is perfectly okay.

This book is a practical guide for thriving in a world that favors early risers. It is designed to help you optimize your life by working *with* your biology, not against it.

We will help you redefine what a "morning routine" means. A morning routine is not something that happens at 6 AM. It is the set of actions you take during the first few hours after you wake up—whether that's at 7 AM, 9 AM, or even 11 AM.

The goal is not to wake up early. The goal is to wake up *well*.

Here is what we will not do:

- We will not demand you wake up at 5 AM.
- We will not use guilt or shame as motivation.
- We will not offer rigid, minute-by-minute schedules.

Instead, here is what we will cover:

- **Understanding the Science:** We will look at why your body works the way it does and why fighting it is counterproductive.
- **Dismantling the Guilt:** We will challenge the irrational beliefs that connect early rising with virtue and success.
- **The Night Owl Advantage:** We will explore the unique strengths that often come with being an evening type, such as increased creativity and deep focus.
- **Building Your Ideal Routine:** We will provide flexible frameworks for starting your day slowly, managing sleep inertia, and protecting your peak energy hours. We will shift the focus from *time management* to *energy management*.
- **The Evening Prep:** We will show you how a successful morning for a night owl actually begins the night before.
- **Navigating the 9-to-5:** We will offer practical strategies for surviving early meetings and mandatory start times when you can't control your schedule.

This is not about doing less. It's about doing things smarter, according to your own rhythm.

What is the Anti-5AM?

The Anti-5AM is not an organization. It's a mindset. It's a movement for everyone who has ever felt shamed by productivity advice that ignores their reality.

It's about recognizing that the traditional rules of success were written by only one type of person. It's time to write new rules.

The core principles of the Anti-5AM are:

1. **Biology over Bravado:** We respect our chronotype. We do not believe that suffering is a prerequisite for success.
2. **Energy over Hours:** We focus on managing our energy levels and optimizing our peak performance windows, rather than obsessing over the clock.
3. **Results over Routine:** We judge success by the outcomes we achieve, not by the time we wake up.
4. **Self-Acceptance over Self-Criticism:** We stop apologizing for how we are wired. We embrace our night owl nature as a strength.

Welcome to the union. You don't have to wake up early to join. You just have to be willing to challenge the myths that have kept you feeling tired and frustrated.

It's time to reclaim your morning, on your schedule. We're glad you slept in.

Reflecting on Your Rhythm

Take a moment to consider your own energy patterns and your relationship with the morning.

When do you naturally feel most focused and creative during the day?

(Space for reflection)

If you didn't have to set an alarm for a week, what time would your body naturally fall asleep and wake up?

(Space for reflection)

What feelings come up when you hit the snooze button or wake up later than society expects? (e.g., guilt, shame, frustration)

(Space for reflection)

How much time and energy have you spent feeling guilty about not waking up earlier? What beliefs drive that guilt? (e.g., "I must wake up early to be successful.")

(Space for reflection)

Key Ideas to take home

- The guilt and shame associated with waking up later are often worse than the physical tiredness.
- The cultural obsession with early rising (the 5AM Lie) ignores the fact that nearly half the population is not suited for it.
- The belief that early rising is morally superior or necessary for success is irrational.
- Night owls are not lazy; they have a different biological wiring, known as their chronotype.
- You cannot force yourself to become a morning person if you are genetically wired to be an evening person.

- The goal is to work with your biology, focusing on energy management over time management, to create routines that support your well-being.

Armed with this understanding of the cultural pressures and the reality of your biology, we can begin to dismantle the specific myths that keep us trapped in this cycle of exhaustion.

Chapter 1: The Myth of the Moral Morning

We have a strange habit of attaching morality to simple behaviors. We think some foods are "good" and others are "bad." We think being busy is "virtuous" and resting is "lazy." But perhaps the strangest moral judgment we make is about sleep.

Think about the language we use. "The early bird gets the worm." "Early to bed and early to rise makes a man healthy, wealthy, and wise."

These sayings aren't just observations; they are judgments. They imply that if you are *not* an early bird, you won't get the worm. If you stay up late and wake up late, you are destined to be sick, poor, and foolish.

This is the Myth of the Moral Morning. It's the belief that the time you wake up determines your character. It suggests that people who wake up at 5 AM are inherently better, more disciplined, and more deserving of success than those who wake up at 9 AM.

Let's be direct: This is nonsense. It's irrational thinking, and it's causing a lot of unnecessary misery. If you believe your worth is tied to your alarm clock, you are setting yourself up for frustration. This chapter is about dismantling that myth, understanding where it came from, and recognizing the damage it causes.

Early rising isn't the secret to success

We tend to admire what we see. And what we see in the media are CEOs, athletes, and influencers bragging about their pre-dawn routines. They post about their 4:30 AM workouts and their quiet hours of meditation before the sun rises. The message seems clear: *This* is the secret to their success.

But this creates a logical error. We confuse correlation with causation. Just because some successful people wake up early doesn't mean waking up early *causes* their success.

It's like noticing that many basketball players are tall. Playing basketball does not make you tall. Being tall makes you better suited for basketball. Similarly, if you are naturally a morning person, waking up early works for you. You are playing to your strengths.

But what about successful night owls? They exist, and there are many of them. Leaders in science, art, and business often keep late hours. When they achieve great things, it's usually during their peak hours—late afternoon or evening. They rarely post about sleeping until 10 AM because society has taught them to hide it.

The belief that early rising is superior relies on a few core irrational ideas, often expressed as "shoulds."

- "I *should* wake up earlier if I want to be successful."
- "I *should* have more willpower in the morning."
- "I *shouldn't* feel so tired when the alarm goes off."

When we use the word "should," we are often imposing an external rule on ourselves without questioning it. And when we fail to live up to that rule—because our biology resists it—we don't blame the rule. We blame ourselves.

Let's challenge these beliefs.

Irrational Belief #1: "I must wake up early to be disciplined."

Discipline is not about forcing yourself to do something painful and unnatural. Discipline is about consistently working toward your goals in a sustainable way. If you force yourself to wake up at 5 AM but are too exhausted to work effectively, that's not discipline; it's self-sabotage. True discipline for a night owl might mean protecting evening hours for focused work and structuring the morning to start slowly.

Irrational Belief #2: "If I sleep later, I am lazy."

Laziness is an unwillingness to work or use energy. It has nothing to do with your sleep schedule. If you sleep from midnight to 8 AM, and then work productively for eight hours, you are not lazy. The amount of sleep you need, and when you need it, is biological. Demanding that you must change this is irrational.

When we cling to the myth of the moral morning, we value the appearance of productivity over actual productivity.

The History of the "Early Bird" Obsession

If biology doesn't dictate that early rising is better, where did this obsession come from? It's largely cultural and historical.

The Agricultural Roots

In farming societies, life revolved around the sun. Daylight was a limited resource. You had to wake up early to tend the crops and feed the animals. In this context, "the early bird gets the worm" made practical sense.

We inherited this mindset. But most of us are no longer milking cows.

The Industrial Revolution and the Clock

The real shift happened during the Industrial Revolution. Factories needed large numbers of workers to start at the same time to operate machinery efficiently. The clock became the master.

It didn't matter if you were tired. The factory whistle blew, and you had to be there. Early rising became associated with reliability and obedience. Sleeping in became associated with lack of discipline. The 9-to-5 schedule was designed for the convenience of factory owners, not the optimization of human biology. It favored morning types and punished evening types.

The Knowledge Economy: A Mismatch

We now live in the Knowledge Economy. Work is no longer about assembling parts on a line. It's about creativity, problem-solving, and critical thinking. This type of work depends heavily on brain function.

Here is the mismatch: We are using an Industrial Age schedule to solve Knowledge Economy problems.

If a factory worker is operating at 70% capacity, they can still assemble the part. But if a programmer, writer, or strategist is operating at 70% capacity, the quality of their work suffers significantly.

In today's world, *when* you work is less important than *how well* you work. We have electric lights and the internet. We can work effectively at any time. Yet, we cling to the outdated belief that the hours before noon are the only ones that count.

We are trying to use a 200-year-old operating system for modern hardware. It's time for an upgrade.

The Mental and Physical Costs of "Sleep Bullying"

What happens when you try to force a night owl to become a morning person? It's not just uncomfortable; it's harmful.

We can call this *Sleep Bullying*. It's the constant pressure from society, employers, and even ourselves to conform to an unnatural sleep schedule.

The costs are real.

Physical Health Impacts

When you constantly fight your internal clock, you are putting your body in a state of chronic stress. You accumulate *sleep debt*. This is linked to a host of health problems:

- **Weakened Immune System:** You may find yourself getting sick more often.
- **Metabolic Issues:** Chronic sleep deprivation and misalignment can increase the risk of weight gain, diabetes, and cardiovascular problems.
- **Chronic Fatigue:** You are never truly rested because you are constantly cutting your sleep short.

It is ironic that many people wake up early to "improve their health" (like going to the gym), but the act of waking up too early is actually damaging their health.

Mental Health Impacts

The emotional toll of sleep bullying is often the heaviest burden.

- **Anxiety and Depression:** There is a strong link between chronotype misalignment and mood disorders. Night owls forced onto early schedules are more likely to report symptoms of depression. Part of this is biological, but part of it is the constant feeling of failure and guilt.
- **Brain Fog and Irritability:** When you are exhausted, small problems feel like big problems. You struggle to concentrate and make decisions.
- **Burnout:** You are pushing yourself harder just to keep up. You are using caffeine and willpower to force your brain to function when it wants to rest. This is not sustainable.

Consider the case of a teacher who naturally thrives in the evening. However, they must be in the classroom by 7:30 AM. They wake up at 6 AM feeling foggy. They get through the morning on adrenaline and coffee. By the afternoon, they crash. They constantly feel like they are failing their students and themselves. They believe, "I must be doing something wrong, because this shouldn't be this hard."

The reality is, the job *is* that hard when you are fighting your biology every single day. The belief that they *must* adapt, rather than acknowledging the conflict, is what fuels the misery.

The Toxic Side of Productivity Culture

The self-help industry is supposed to make us feel better. But often, it does the opposite.

Productivity Culture, in its current toxic form, is obsessed with optimization, efficiency, and "hacking" our biology. It promotes the idea that humans should operate like machines. The 5AM phenomenon is a perfect example. It sells a fantasy that you can achieve anything if you just sacrifice sleep and comfort.

This is where self-help becomes self-harm.

The Glorification of Sleep Deprivation

You hear people bragging, "I only need four hours of sleep." This is almost always a dangerous misunderstanding of biology. Glorifying sleep deprivation is like glorifying malnutrition.

The "Perfect Routine" Trap

Toxic productivity promotes the idea that there is a "perfect routine." If you just meditate, exercise, journal, and drink green juice before 8 AM, you will be successful.

When night owls try to adopt these routines, they fail. Not because the routines are bad, but because the timing is wrong. Trying to meditate when your body is screaming for sleep is pointless.

The Denial of Individuality

The most toxic aspect of this culture is its denial of human variation. It promotes a one-size-fits-all solution. It tells you that if you cannot follow the prescribed routine, the fault lies with you. Your willpower is weak.

This takes a systemic problem (the rigid structure of society) and turns it into a personal failure. It makes you feel ashamed of your biology.

True self-improvement is not about forcing yourself into a mold. It's about understanding how you are wired and creating a life that works for you.

It's time to reject the toxic productivity advice that makes you feel miserable. It's time to recognize that the myth of the moral morning is just that—a myth.

Exercise: Challenging Your Morning "Shoulds"

This exercise will help you identify and challenge the irrational beliefs you hold about mornings and productivity.

1. **Identify the "Shoulds":** Write down the rules you have about waking up and mornings.
   - *Example: I should wake up by 6 AM.*
   - *Example: I shouldn't hit the snooze button.*

   (Space for reflection)

2. **Question the Source:** For each rule, ask yourself: Where did this rule come from? (e.g., parents, a book, social media, cultural expectations).
   - *Example: The idea that successful CEOs wake up early.*

(Space for reflection)

3. **Challenge the Validity:** Ask yourself: Is this rule universally true for everyone? Is there evidence that contradicts it?
    - *Example: No, many successful people wake up later. Waking up early doesn't guarantee success.*

(Space for reflection)

4. **Reframe with Reality:** Rewrite the rule based on your own reality and needs.
    - *Example: I want to wake up feeling rested so I can be productive during my peak hours, regardless of the time.*

(Space for reflection)

Key Takeaways

- We have attached a moral value to waking up early, leading to unnecessary guilt and shame.
- The belief that early rising is essential for success is an irrational belief, often expressed as "shoulds."
- The obsession with early rising stems from the Industrial Revolution and is outdated in the modern Knowledge Economy.
- "Sleep Bullying"—forcing an unnatural sleep schedule—has significant physical and mental costs, including sleep deprivation and burnout.
- Toxic productivity culture often promotes one-size-fits-all solutions that ignore individual differences, turning self-help into self-harm.

Having cleared this conceptual space around the morality of mornings, we can now look closer at the actual reasons why we sleep the way we do.

Chapter 2: It's Not Laziness, It's Biology (Chronotypes 101)

We often mistake biological differences for behavioral choices.

If someone needs glasses, we don't accuse them of not trying hard enough to see. We understand that their eyesight is different. We give them glasses. We don't demand they squint until they get a headache.

Yet, when it comes to sleep, we do exactly that. We tell night owls to "just try harder" to wake up early. We treat their natural rhythm as a bad habit that needs to be broken.

This approach is fundamentally flawed. It ignores the reality of human biology. You are not lazy, disorganized, or unmotivated because you struggle with mornings. You are simply wired differently.

Understanding how this wiring works is crucial. When you stop blaming yourself and start understanding your biology, you can begin to build strategies that actually work.

Larks, Hummingbirds, and Owls

Scientists who study sleep use the term *chronotype* to describe a person's natural tendency to sleep and wake at certain times. Your chronotype is determined by your internal biological clock, also known as your circadian rhythm.

Think of your circadian rhythm as a 24-hour cycle that regulates sleep, hormone production, and body temperature. Everyone's clock runs on a roughly 24-hour cycle, but everyone's clock is set slightly differently.

Generally, people fall into three main categories:

1. Larks (Morning Types)

Larks are the "early birds." They naturally wake up early (around 6 AM or earlier) and feel most alert in the morning. Their energy peaks around noon. They find it easy to fall asleep early (around 9 PM or 10 PM). Larks thrive in a traditional 9-to-5 world.

2. Owls (Evening Types)

Owls are the opposite. They struggle to wake up early. Waking up at 7 AM can feel like the middle of the night. Their energy levels are low in the morning and increase throughout the day, peaking in the afternoon or evening. They find it difficult to fall asleep early and often go to bed after midnight.

3. Hummingbirds (Intermediate Types)

The majority of people fall somewhere in the middle. They are the Hummingbirds. They can adapt to a traditional schedule (waking up around 7-8 AM and going to bed around 11 PM) without much difficulty.

It's important to understand this is a spectrum. Roughly 15-25% of the population are strong night owls. But when you combine Owls and later-leaning Hummingbirds, approximately 40-60% of the population is not naturally inclined to wake up very early.

The key takeaway is this: Your chronotype is real. It is not a preference or a habit. It is a biological reality.

The Genetic Basis of the Night Owl

For a long time, night owls were told that their sleep patterns were a result of bad habits—too much screen time or poor discipline. While these things can affect your sleep, they do not determine your chronotype.

Your chronotype is largely genetic.

Research has identified specific genes, often called "clock genes," that regulate our circadian rhythms. These genes determine whether your internal clock runs slightly faster (making you a Lark) or slightly slower (making you an Owl).

The Hormonal Connection

The difference between Larks and Owls is visible in their hormone levels. *Melatonin*, the hormone that makes you sleepy, is released later in the evening for Owls than for Larks. And it stays in their system later into the morning.

This is crucial. If you are a night owl and you try to wake up at 6 AM, your body is still producing melatonin. Your brain is still in "sleep mode." It's biologically equivalent to a Lark waking up at 3 AM.

Similarly, trying to force yourself to sleep at 10 PM won't work if your body isn't producing melatonin yet. You will just lie awake, frustrated.

Why Does This Variation Exist?

Scientists believe this variation provided a survival advantage for early human groups. If a tribe had both Larks and Owls, someone would always be awake or lightly sleeping to watch for danger. The Larks guarded the camp in the early morning, and the Owls guarded it late at night.

It was a cooperative system. But in modern society, we have turned it into a competition, insisting that the Lark way is the only way.

Accepting Your Reality

Understanding the genetic basis of your chronotype is crucial for self-acceptance. You cannot willpower your way out of your genes.

When you accept this reality, you can stop wasting energy trying to fix something that isn't broken.

Think about a person who spent years trying to force themselves into an early routine. They tried every trick: cold showers, early morning classes. Nothing worked sustainably. They always felt exhausted and reverted to their natural pattern. They felt like a failure. When this person learned about chronotypes, it was a revelation. "It's not that I'm weak," they realized. "It's that I've been following the wrong instructions."

Why Night Owls Take Longer to "Boot Up"

You've probably experienced this: You wake up, but you don't feel awake. Your brain is foggy. You feel clumsy, slow, and irritable. It's like trying to drive a car with the parking brake on.

This phenomenon is called *sleep inertia*. It's the transitional state between sleep and full wakefulness.

Everyone experiences sleep inertia, but it tends to be much worse and last much longer for night owls, especially when they are forced to wake up early.

Why Does It Happen?

When you wake up, your brain needs time to reboot. Different parts of the brain wake up at different speeds. The prefrontal cortex—the area responsible for complex thinking and decision-making—is the last part to come online.

For Larks, this process might take 15 to 30 minutes. For Owls woken up early, it can last for two to four hours.

The Impact of Sleep Inertia

During this period, your cognitive abilities are significantly impaired. Your reaction time is slower. Your memory is fuzzy.

In fact, the cognitive impairment during severe sleep inertia is comparable to being mildly intoxicated.

Think about the implications. If you are a night owl forced to start work at 8 AM, you are likely spending the first few hours of your workday in a state of impaired cognitive function.

This is why the traditional advice to "tackle your most important task first thing in the morning" is terrible advice for night owls. It sets them up for failure.

The key is to accept that you need a "boot-up" period. Instead of jumping straight into demanding tasks, you need a routine that allows your brain to gradually warm up.

Social Jetlag

We usually associate jetlag with travel across time zones. But night owls experience a form of jetlag every single week, without leaving home. This is called *social jetlag*.

Social jetlag is the difference between your biological clock (when your body wants to sleep) and your social clock (when work or school demands you to be awake).

The Weekly Cycle of Misery

Here is how it typically plays out for a night owl with a standard job:

- **Monday to Friday (The Social Clock):** You force yourself to wake up early, say at 7 AM, even though your body wants to sleep until 9 AM. You accumulate sleep debt throughout the week.

- **The Weekend (The Biological Clock):** You "sleep in" on Saturday and Sunday to catch up. You shift back toward your natural rhythm.
- **Monday Morning (The Shock):** The alarm goes off at 7 AM again. Your body, which has just adjusted to the later schedule, is forced to jump back two hours. This is why Monday mornings feel so brutal. You are literally jetlagged.

The Costs of Social Jetlag

Social jetlag is not just uncomfortable. It has serious long-term consequences. Research has linked chronic social jetlag to:

- Increased risk of obesity and metabolic disorders.

- Higher rates of caffeine consumption.

- Increased risk of depression and anxiety.

- Poorer work performance.

The ideal solution is to have a work schedule that aligns with your chronotype. However, this is not always possible. If you are stuck in a rigid schedule, the goal is to minimize the shift between your weekday and weekend schedules.

Recognizing the impact of social jetlag can help you understand why you feel so chronically tired and help you make informed choices about your schedule. The fundamental problem is that society treats the morning chronotype as the default. Recognizing the reality of biology is the first step toward changing this narrative.

Exercise: Finding Your Chronotype

While online quizzes can give you a rough idea, the best way to determine your chronotype is by observing your natural rhythm.

Step 1: Reflect on Your Energy Levels

Think about your typical day.

- When do you feel most energized and focused? (e.g., Morning, Afternoon, Evening)

  (Space for reflection)

- When do you feel most tired and sluggish?

  (Space for reflection)

Step 2: Observe Your Natural Sleep Patterns

The best time to do this is during a vacation when you don't have to set an alarm. If that's not possible, look at your weekend patterns.

- When do you naturally start to feel sleepy in the evening?

  (Space for reflection)

- If you didn't set an alarm, what time would you naturally wake up?

  (Space for reflection)

Step 3: Assess Your Morning Experience

- How do you feel during the first hour after waking up on a weekday? (e.g., Alert, Foggy, Irritable)

  (Space for reflection)

- How long does it take for you to feel fully awake and functional?

  (Space for reflection)

Interpreting Your Results:

- If you prefer to sleep early and wake early, and feel most energized in the morning, you are likely a **Lark**.
- If you prefer to sleep late and wake late, and feel most energized in the evening, you are likely an **Owl**.
- If you fall somewhere in the middle, you are likely a **Hummingbird**.

Key Ideas from Chapter 2

- Your chronotype (being a Lark, Owl, or Hummingbird) is your body's natural tendency to sleep and wake at certain times.

- Your chronotype is largely genetic and biological. It is not a choice or a reflection of your discipline.

- Night owls have different hormonal patterns, with melatonin being released later and staying longer in their system.

- Sleep inertia (the morning fog) is a transitional state between sleep and wakefulness, and it lasts much longer for night owls.

- Social jetlag is the difference between your biological clock and your social clock. It contributes to chronic fatigue and health problems.

With this foundation laid within you, we can now shift our perspective from seeing the night owl pattern as a liability to recognizing its unique advantages.

Chapter 3: The Night Owl Advantage

For too long, the conversation about night owls has focused on the negatives: the difficulty waking up, the morning fog, the clash with the 9-to-5 world.

We are told we are out of sync. We are told we need to fix ourselves.

But what if being a night owl isn't a problem to be solved? What if it's actually an advantage?

If you've spent your life believing you are inherently flawed because of your sleep schedule, this idea might seem radical. But the reality is that evening types possess unique strengths that morning types often lack.

This chapter is about redefining the narrative. It's about identifying and harnessing the Night Owl Advantage. It's about shifting from a mindset of deficit to a mindset of strength.

Identifying the Unique Strengths of Late Risers

When we look at the research on chronotypes, a fascinating pattern emerges. While Larks often excel in structured environments, Owls tend to shine in areas requiring creativity, deep thinking, and sustained focus.

Let's explore some of these strengths.

1. Enhanced Creativity and "Out-of-the-Box" Thinking

There is a strong link between evening chronotypes and creativity. Night owls tend to be more adept at *divergent thinking*—the ability to generate multiple solutions to a problem and see connections between seemingly unrelated ideas.

Why is this? The evening hours provide a quieter, less structured environment. The distractions of the day have faded away. The mind is free to wander.

2. Deep Focus and Concentration (At the Right Time)

While night owls struggle with focus in the morning, they often experience periods of intense concentration and "flow" in the afternoon and evening. This allows them to dive deeply into complex tasks.

Morning types often experience a dip in energy in the afternoon. Night owls, on the other hand, are just ramping up.

3. Cognitive Strengths: Analytical Thinking

Research suggests that night owls may have advantages in certain areas of intelligence, particularly in inductive reasoning and analytical thinking. They tend to perform well on tasks that require complex problem-solving. This doesn't mean night owls are "smarter"; it means their cognitive strengths peak at different times.

4. Stamina and Endurance

Night owls often exhibit greater mental stamina later in the day. While Larks might be tired by 8 PM, Owls are often still going strong. This allows them to capitalize on the quiet evening hours for productive work or creative projects.

The Irrational Belief: "My Peak Hours Don't Count"

Many night owls discount their strengths because they happen at the "wrong" time. They believe that work done in the evening is somehow less valuable than work done in the morning.

This is an irrational belief rooted in the Myth of the Moral Morning. If you produce brilliant work at 10 PM, it is just as valuable as brilliant work produced at 10 AM.

The key is to recognize these strengths and structure your life to utilize them.

Redefining "Peak Performance" Windows

Productivity advice often talks about "Peak Performance Windows." This is the time of day when your energy, focus, and cognitive abilities are at their highest.

The problem is that most advice assumes this window is between 9 AM and noon. For a night owl, this assumption is disastrous.

The Night Owl Performance Curve

Let's look at the typical energy pattern of a night owl:

- **Morning (7 AM - 10 AM): The Trough.** This is the period of high sleep inertia. Energy is low. Focus is scattered. This is the worst time for demanding cognitive work.
- **Late Morning/Early Afternoon (10 AM - 2 PM): The Ramp-Up.** Sleep inertia begins to fade. Energy levels gradually increase. This is a good time for moderately demanding tasks.
- **Late Afternoon/Evening (2 PM - 8 PM): The Peak.** Energy levels are high. Focus is sharp. Creativity is sparked. This is the ideal time for deep work and complex problem-solving.
- **Late Evening (8 PM - Midnight): The Second Wind.** Many night owls experience a second burst of energy and creativity late in the evening.

The Strategy: Aligning Tasks with Energy

The key to maximizing your productivity as a night owl is to move from *time management* to *energy management*.

Time management is about allocating hours. It assumes every hour is equal. Energy management is about aligning tasks with your energy levels. It recognizes that an hour of peak time is worth three hours of low energy time.

Here is how to redefine your approach:

1. **Protect Your Peak:** Identify your peak performance window and treat it as sacred. Schedule your most important and demanding tasks during this time.
2. **Manage Your Trough:** Accept that your morning hours will be slow. Use this time for low-demand tasks: checking email, organizing your workspace, or gentle movement. Do not schedule high-stakes decisions during this time if you can avoid it.
3. **Utilize Your Ramp-Up:** As your energy increases, gradually increase the complexity of your tasks.

Consider a software developer who works a 9-to-5 job. They used to try to do their most complex coding in the morning because that's what the productivity gurus advised. They struggled and felt frustrated.

When they redefined their peak performance window, they changed their approach. They used the morning for administrative tasks and code reviews. They reserved the afternoon (their peak) for intensive coding. The result? They produced better code in less time and felt less stressed.

The challenge is not to change your energy pattern. The challenge is to honor it.

Case Studies of Successful Night Owls

The world is full of successful people who rejected the early bird mantra and embraced their night owl nature. Success is not just about fame and fortune. Success is about living a fulfilling, productive life on your own terms.

Let's look at some examples of people who harnessed the Night Owl Advantage.

The Entrepreneur Who Built a Business After Dark

One entrepreneur struggled to launch their business while working a traditional day job. They tried waking up early to work on their side hustle, but their brain simply wouldn't cooperate.

They decided to embrace their biology. They used their evenings, from 9 PM to 1 AM, as their primary work time. During these quiet hours, they found the focus and creativity they needed to develop their product. Within a year, they were able to quit their day job and run their successful business—on their own schedule.

The Artist Who Found Their Flow at Midnight

A visual artist felt constant pressure to produce work during "normal" business hours. They would sit in their studio during the day, feeling blocked and uninspired. They believed they lacked discipline.

When they allowed themselves to follow their natural rhythm, everything changed. They started working late in the evening. They found that the solitude of the night unlocked their creativity. They produced their best work during these hours, leading to greater satisfaction.

The Parent Who Redefined "Quality Time"

A busy parent who is a natural night owl felt guilty about their low energy levels in the morning. They struggled to be cheerful and engaged with their children before school.

They decided to shift their perspective. They accepted that their mornings would be slow and focused on creating a calm, predictable routine. They reserved their energy for the evenings, when they were more alert and playful. They created evening rituals—reading stories, playing games, having deep conversations. They realized that being present is more important than the time of day it happens.

These stories highlight a common theme: Success came not from conforming to the early bird standard, but from intentionally rejecting it and optimizing their lives around their biology.

"Waking Up Early" to "Waking Up Well"

The obsession with "waking up early" is a trap. It focuses on the wrong metric. The time you wake up is irrelevant. What matters is how you feel when you wake up and what you do with your waking hours.

It's time to change the goal. The goal is not to wake up early. The goal is to wake up *well*.

What does it mean to wake up well?

- **Waking Up Rested:** It means getting enough sleep to feel physically and mentally restored. For night owls, this often means sleeping later than society dictates.
- **Waking Up Without Guilt:** It means separating your self-worth from your alarm clock. It means rejecting the shame associated with sleeping in.
- **Waking Up Intentionally:** It means starting your day with a clear sense of purpose, rather than rushing into a frenzy of activity.

- **Waking Up Gradually:** It means respecting your body's need for a transition period (sleep inertia) and creating a routine that allows you to start slowly.

The Anti-5AM approach is about optimization, not conformity. It's about finding the rhythm that maximizes your energy, creativity, and well-being.

When you make this shift, you unlock your true potential. You stop wasting energy fighting yourself and start using that energy to build the life you want.

Exercise: Mapping Your Energy Curve

This exercise will help you identify your peak performance windows and optimize your schedule.

1. **Track Your Energy:** For the next three days, keep a simple log of your energy levels throughout the day. Use a scale of 1 to 10 (1 = exhausted, 10 = energized). Record your energy level every two hours.

   (Space for tracking)

2. **Identify Your Patterns:** Look at your log.
   - When is your energy consistently the highest? This is your **Peak**.
   - When is your energy consistently the lowest? This is your **Trough**.
   - When is your energy rising or falling? This is your **Ramp-Up/Ramp-Down**.

   (Space for reflection)

3. **Analyze Your Current Schedule:** Look at how you are currently spending your time.

o Are you doing demanding tasks during your Trough?

o Are you wasting your Peak hours on low-value activities?

(Space for reflection)

4. **Redesign Your Day:** Based on your energy curve, brainstorm ways you can realign your tasks.
    o How can you protect your Peak for your most important work?

    o What low-demand tasks can you shift to your Trough?

(Space for planning)

Key Takeaways

- Night owls possess unique strengths, including enhanced creativity, deep focus, analytical thinking, and stamina during later hours.

- It is irrational to believe that work done in the evening is less valuable than work done in the morning.

- Peak performance windows for night owls are typically in the late afternoon and evening.

- The key to productivity is to align your tasks with your energy levels (energy management), rather than just managing your time.

- The goal should be to "wake up well"—rested, without guilt, and intentionally—rather than "waking up early."

Now that you've explored this territory of your biology and strengths, we can start building the framework for a routine that actually works for you.

Chapter 4: Redefining "Morning"

When you hear the phrase "morning routine," what comes to mind?

You probably picture someone waking up before the sun, perhaps drinking a green smoothie, meditating on a cushion, and then effortlessly starting their workday. It's a peaceful image. It's also completely unrealistic for most night owls.

The traditional concept of "morning" is tied to the clock. It's defined as the early hours of the day, usually between 6 AM and 9 AM. If you don't wake up during that window, you feel like you've missed the morning entirely.

This belief causes a lot of problems. It makes you feel rushed, guilty, and disorganized. If you wake up at 9:30 AM, you might feel like it's too late to have a routine. You just jump straight into your day, feeling scattered and reactive.

It's time to challenge this definition. It's time to decouple the idea of a "morning routine" from the time on the clock.

This chapter is about redefining what "morning" means for you. It's about creating a structure that supports your biology and sets you up for success, no matter when your day begins.

Your "Morning" Starts When You Wake Up

This is the core principle of the Anti-5AM

Your morning starts when you wake up, whether that's 7 AM or 11 AM.

This might sound obvious, but it's a profound shift in mindset.

If you wake up at 10 AM, then 10 AM is your morning. You have the same right to a thoughtful, intentional routine as someone who wakes up at 6 AM.

The belief that you *must* wake up early to have a proper morning is an irrational belief. It's based on the assumption that the early hours are somehow better or more valuable than the later hours. As we discussed in Chapter 1, this is simply not true.

When you cling to the traditional definition of morning, you create unnecessary stress.

Consider a freelance writer who naturally sleeps from 2 AM to 10 AM. For years, they felt guilty about this schedule. They believed, "I *should* be up by 8 AM. It's embarrassing to start my day so late."

When they woke up at 10 AM, they felt rushed. They skipped breakfast, immediately started checking emails, and felt anxious about the "lost time." By noon, they felt drained and unproductive.

When they redefined their morning, everything changed. They accepted that 10 AM was their starting point. They created a routine: 10:00 AM wake up, 10:15 AM coffee and reading (not email), 10:45 AM shower and breakfast, 11:30 AM start work.

By giving themselves permission to have a morning routine at 10 AM, they reduced their stress and improved their focus. They stopped apologizing for their schedule and started optimizing it.

Dismantling the "Late Riser Guilt"

The biggest obstacle to redefining your morning is guilt. You might feel like you are breaking a rule or doing something wrong by waking up later.

Let's confront this guilt directly. Ask yourself:

- Why do I feel guilty about waking up later?

- Who says that waking up early is better?
- Am I getting enough sleep?
- Am I productive during my waking hours?

If you are getting enough sleep and meeting your responsibilities, then the time you wake up is irrelevant. The guilt is a result of internalizing the Myth of the Moral Morning.

Remember: The goal is not to conform to society's schedule. The goal is to create a schedule that works for you.

When you accept your natural rhythm, you free up the mental energy you were wasting on guilt and frustration. You can then use that energy to build a routine that supports your well-being.

The "First Three Hours" Principle

If "morning" isn't a time on the clock, what is it?

We define it as the crucial transition period between sleep and full engagement with the world. This leads us to the *"First Three Hours" Principle*.

This principle states that the actions you take during the first three hours after waking have a disproportionate impact on the rest of your day. They set the tone, stabilize your energy, and prepare your brain for focused work.

It doesn't matter if those three hours are 5 AM to 8 AM or 10 AM to 1 PM. What matters is what you do with them.

Why Three Hours?

For night owls, the first three hours are especially critical because of sleep inertia (the morning fog we discussed in Chapter 2). Your brain needs time to gradually boot up. Rushing this process is counterproductive.

The First Three Hours can be broken down into three phases:

Phase 1: The Awakening (0-60 minutes)

This phase is about gently transitioning from sleep to wakefulness. The goal is to minimize stress and clear the initial fog.

- **What to do:** Hydrate, get some light, gentle movement (stretching), basic hygiene.
- **What to avoid:** Checking email, social media, stressful conversations, intense exercise.

Phase 2: The Alignment (60-120 minutes)

This phase is about aligning yourself with your priorities and preparing for the day. Your brain is starting to warm up.

- **What to do:** Eat a nourishing breakfast, review your goals, light reading, meditation or journaling (if that works for you).
- **What to avoid:** Deep work, complex decision-making.

Phase 3: The Launchpad (120-180 minutes)

This phase is about transitioning into your workday. Your sleep inertia should be mostly gone, and you are approaching your peak energy levels.

- **What to do:** Start with moderate-demand tasks, organize your workspace, prepare for deep work.
- **What to avoid:** Getting distracted by low-priority tasks.

Flexibility is Key

The First Three Hours Principle is a framework, not a rigid schedule. Some days you might need more time in Phase 1. Some days you might move faster into Phase 3.

The key is to be intentional about how you use this time. Don't let it be consumed by default activities like scrolling on your phone or reacting to other people's demands.

When you focus on the *actions* you take upon waking, rather than the *time* you wake up, you regain control over your day.

Time Management to Energy Management

Traditional productivity advice is obsessed with time management. It's all about maximizing every minute, cramming more tasks into the day, and adhering to rigid schedules.

This approach works reasonably well for morning people, whose energy levels align with the traditional workday. But for night owls, it's a recipe for burnout.

Why? Because time management assumes that every hour is equal. It assumes that an hour at 8 AM is the same as an hour at 8 PM.

As a night owl, you know this is false. An hour during your peak time (late afternoon or evening) is far more valuable than an hour during your trough (early morning).

It's time to shift your focus from *time management* to *energy management*.

Energy management is about optimizing your cognitive resources, not just your schedule. It's about recognizing when you are most effective and aligning your tasks accordingly.

The Principles of Energy Management

Here are the core principles of energy management for night owls:

1. **Know Your Curve:** Understand your daily energy patterns. (We covered this in Chapter 3). Know when your peaks and troughs occur.

2. **Align Tasks with Energy:** Match the demands of the task with the energy you have available.
    - **High Energy (Peak):** Deep work, complex problem-solving, creativity, important decisions.
    - **Medium Energy (Ramp-Up/Ramp-Down):** Emails, meetings, moderate tasks, planning.
    - **Low Energy (Trough):** Administrative tasks, organizing, resting, gentle movement.
3. **Protect Your Peak:** Treat your peak hours as sacred. Minimize distractions and interruptions during this time.
4. **Respect Your Trough:** Accept that you will have periods of low energy. Don't try to force productivity during these times. Use them for rest and recovery.

The Trap of "Fake Productivity"

When we focus solely on time management, we often fall into the trap of "fake productivity." This is when we are busy but not effective.

For a night owl, trying to do deep work at 8 AM is fake productivity. You might sit at your desk for three hours, but you will only produce one hour's worth of results. And you will feel exhausted afterward.

Energy management encourages you to work smarter, not harder.

Consider a software engineer who needs to write complex code. If they try to do this in the morning (their trough), it takes them four hours and is full of bugs. If they do it in the afternoon (their peak), it takes them two hours and is high quality.

By shifting to energy management, they save two hours and produce better work.

The Power of Acceptance

Energy management requires a high level of self-acceptance. You have to accept that you are not a machine. You cannot operate at 100% capacity all day long.

You have to reject the irrational belief that you *should* be productive 24/7.

When you embrace your natural rhythm, you unlock a more sustainable and effective way of working. You stop fighting your biology and start leveraging it.

Exercise: Designing Your First Three Hours

This exercise will help you create a flexible framework for your morning routine, based on the First Three Hours Principle.

Step 1: Define Your Phases

Based on the descriptions above, brainstorm activities that would fit into each phase for you. Be realistic about your energy levels.

- **Phase 1: The Awakening (0-60 minutes) - Goal: Gentle transition.**
  - *Example: Drink water, stretch for 5 minutes, make coffee.*

(Space for brainstorming)

- **Phase 2: The Alignment (60-120 minutes) - Goal: Prepare for the day.**
  - *Example: Eat breakfast, review my top 3 priorities, read a chapter of a book.*

(Space for brainstorming)

- **Phase 3: The Launchpad (120-180 minutes) - Goal: Transition into work.**
  - *Example: Check emails (time-boxed), organize my desk, start with my easiest task.*

(Space for brainstorming)

Step 2: Identify Potential Obstacles

What might get in the way of executing your First Three Hours?

- *Example: The urge to check my phone immediately.*
- *Example: Family demands or early meetings.*

(Space for reflection)

Step 3: Create Solutions

How can you mitigate these obstacles?

- *Example: Keep my phone out of the bedroom.*
- *Example: Communicate my routine to my family, or adapt the phases to fit the demands.*

(Space for planning)

Key Ideas from Chapter 4

- Your "morning" starts when you wake up, regardless of the time on the clock.

- Reject the guilt associated with waking up later. It is based on irrational beliefs about productivity and morality.

- The "First Three Hours" Principle focuses on the crucial actions taken upon waking, setting the tone for the rest of the day.

- The First Three Hours are divided into three phases: Awakening, Alignment, and Launchpad.

- Shift your focus from time management (maximizing hours) to energy management (optimizing cognitive resources).

- Energy management involves knowing your energy curve and aligning tasks with your energy levels.

Having established these coordinates for your morning, we now turn our attention to the often-overlooked foundation of a successful day: the night before.

Chapter 5: The Night Owl's Secret Weapon

When we think about improving our mornings, we naturally focus on what we do when we wake up. We adjust our alarms, try different breakfast foods, or attempt morning exercise.

But these strategies often fail because they address the symptoms, not the cause. They ignore the fact that a successful morning doesn't start in the morning.

For a night owl, a successful morning begins the night before.

This might seem counterintuitive. After all, the evening is when night owls feel most energized. Why would you want to focus on a routine when you are finally feeling productive?

The answer is simple: The way you end your day determines how you start your next day. If you end your day feeling stressed, disorganized, and overstimulated, you will wake up feeling the same way.

The evening routine is the night owl's secret weapon. It's the foundation for a calm, focused, and productive morning—whenever that morning begins.

A Successful Morning Begins the Night Before

Think of your morning self as a different person from your evening self.

Your evening self is energized, focused, and capable. Your morning self (especially during sleep inertia) is foggy, slow, and easily overwhelmed.

The goal of an evening routine is to use the strength of your evening self to support your morning self. It's about setting yourself up for success when you are least capable of doing so.

When you neglect your evening routine, you are essentially sabotaging your future self. You are leaving messes to clean up, decisions to make, and stressors to manage at a time when your cognitive resources are at their lowest.

The Power of Pre-loading

The core concept here is *pre-loading*. This means doing as much as possible in advance to reduce the friction in the morning.

Imagine waking up to a clean kitchen, knowing exactly what you need to do, and having everything prepared. Now imagine waking up to a sink full of dishes, a cluttered workspace, and an overwhelming to-do list.

The difference in your stress levels and productivity is immense.

Challenging the "I'll Do It Tomorrow" Mindset

Night owls often fall into the trap of procrastination during the day, pushing tasks to the evening. And then, in the evening, they might feel energized and focused on their current work, pushing the preparation tasks to the next morning.

"I'll do it tomorrow" is often based on the irrational belief that "I *should* be able to handle it in the morning." But as we know, the morning is your cognitive low point.

We need to replace this belief with a more realistic one: "I know I struggle in the morning, so I will do everything I can to make it easier for myself now."

This is not about adding more chores to your evening. It's about making strategic choices that improve the quality of your life.

The Power of the "Pre-Morning Prep"

Every decision you make requires mental energy. This is known as *decision fatigue*.

In the morning, when your prefrontal cortex (the decision-making part of your brain) is still booting up, even small decisions can feel overwhelming.

- What should I wear?
- What should I eat for breakfast?
- What should I work on first?

The goal of the "Pre-Morning Prep" is to eliminate as many of these decisions as possible the night before.

Here are the key areas to focus on:

1. Plan Your Priorities (The Top 3)

The most important decision you can make is what you will focus on the next day. Don't try to create a massive to-do list. Just identify the top three most important tasks.

Be specific. Instead of "work on project," write "finish the first draft of the proposal."

Write these down and put them where you will see them in the morning. This eliminates the paralyzing question of "What should I do now?"

2. Prepare Your Fuel (Food and Drink)

Deciding what to eat and preparing it takes time and energy. Minimize this friction.

- **Breakfast:** If you eat breakfast, decide what it will be. Prepare the ingredients. If you make smoothies, put everything in the blender jar the night before.
- **Coffee/Tea:** Set up your coffee maker or kettle. Get your favorite mug ready.
- **Lunch:** Pack your lunch for the next day. This saves time and money, and ensures you eat something nourishing.

3. Prepare Your Environment

The state of your physical environment has a significant impact on your mental state.

- **Tidy Up:** Do a quick tidy of your workspace and living area. Clear the clutter.
- **Prepare Your Gear:** If you exercise, lay out your workout clothes. If you work from home, make sure your desk is ready. If you commute, pack your bag.

4. Choose Your Outfit

This might seem trivial, but deciding what to wear can be a significant source of stress in the morning. Choose your outfit the night before, down to the socks.

The 15-Minute Investment

The Pre-Morning Prep doesn't have to take long. Even 15 minutes of focused preparation can save you an hour of frustration in the morning.

It's about recognizing that small investments of energy in the evening yield large returns in the morning.

Combating "Revenge Bedtime Procrastination"

If you are a night owl, you are probably familiar with this scenario: You know you should go to bed, but you don't want to. You stay up late scrolling on your phone, watching TV, or engaging in hobbies.

This is often called *"Revenge Bedtime Procrastination"*.

The "revenge" part comes from the feeling that the day has stolen your time. You didn't have enough time for yourself during the day, especially if you work a demanding job that forces you to wake up early. So, you reclaim your time at night, sacrificing sleep for leisure.

Why Do We Do It?

Revenge bedtime procrastination is not a sign of poor discipline. It's a response to stress and a lack of autonomy.

For night owls, the evening is the only time they feel truly alive and energized. It's the only time they feel like themselves. It's understandable that they resist ending the day.

The Cost of Revenge

The problem is that this behavior creates a vicious cycle. You stay up late, you wake up exhausted, you struggle through the day, and then you feel even more stressed and desperate for downtime in the evening.

It reinforces the feeling of chronic fatigue and makes it harder to manage your mornings.

How to Combat It

The solution is not to force yourself to go to bed earlier. The solution is to address the underlying needs that drive the behavior.

1. **Schedule Intentional Downtime:** Don't just wait until bedtime to relax. Schedule intentional breaks and leisure activities throughout the day, especially in the early evening. This reduces the feeling of deprivation that fuels the procrastination.
2. **Create a Transition Ritual:** Instead of working until you crash, create a transition ritual that separates your workday from your evening. This could be closing your laptop, changing your clothes, or taking a short walk.
3. **Set Realistic Expectations:** Accept that you cannot do everything. Prioritize the activities that truly recharge you.
4. **Create a Wind-Down Routine (The Closing Ceremony):** This is the next step, and it's crucial for signaling to your brain that it's time to rest.

Techniques for Winding Down

If you expect to go straight from high-intensity work or entertainment to sleep, you are setting yourself up for failure. Your brain needs time to transition.

The *"Closing Ceremony"* is a sequence of actions you take in the hour before bed to calm your nervous system and prepare your body for sleep.

This is especially important for night owls, whose brains tend to be more active in the evening.

Here are the key components of an effective Closing Ceremony:

1. Minimize Blue Light Exposure

The blue light emitted by screens (phones, tablets, computers, TVs) interferes with the production of melatonin, the hormone that makes you sleepy.

- **The Digital Sunset:** Set a firm time to turn off all screens at least one hour before bed.

- **Use Blue Light Filters:** If you must use screens, use blue light filters or glasses.

2. Calm Your Mind

If your mind is racing with thoughts and anxieties, you won't be able to sleep.

- **Brain Dump:** Write down everything that is on your mind—to-do lists, worries, ideas. Get them out of your head and onto paper.
- **Gentle Relaxation:** Engage in calming activities like reading a physical book (not a thriller), listening to calming music or a podcast, light stretching, or meditation.

3. Optimize Your Sleep Environment

Your bedroom should be a sanctuary for sleep.

- **Keep it Cool:** The optimal temperature for sleep is around 65 degrees Fahrenheit (18 degrees Celsius).
- **Keep it Dark:** Use blackout curtains or an eye mask to block out all light. Even small amounts of light can disrupt your sleep.
- **Keep it Quiet:** Use earplugs or a white noise machine to block out disruptive sounds.

4. Consistency is Key

The Closing Ceremony is most effective when you do it consistently. It trains your brain to associate these activities with sleep.

A Note on Sleep Aids

While many people turn to sleep aids (like melatonin supplements or medications), they should be used with caution and under the guidance of a healthcare professional. Behavioral changes, like the

Closing Ceremony, are often more effective and sustainable in the long run.

By investing in your evening routine, you are investing in the quality of your sleep and the quality of your life. You are taking control of your rhythm and setting yourself up for a better morning.

Exercise: Building Your Evening Routine

This exercise will help you design a personalized evening routine that supports your morning success.

Step 1: Design Your Pre-Morning Prep (15-30 minutes)

List the specific actions you will take to minimize decisions in the morning.

- **Priorities:** How will you identify and record your Top 3 tasks?

  (Space for planning)

- **Fuel:** What will you prepare for breakfast/lunch?

  (Space for planning)

- **Environment:** What will you tidy up? What gear will you prepare?

  (Space for planning)

Step 2: Combatting Procrastination

Reflect on your current evening habits.

- Do you engage in Revenge Bedtime Procrastination? If so, what triggers it?

  (Space for reflection)

- How can you schedule intentional downtime earlier in the evening?

  (Space for planning)

Step 3: Designing Your Closing Ceremony (60 minutes before bed)

Create a sequence of actions to help you wind down.

- **Digital Sunset:** What time will you turn off screens?

  (Space for planning)

- **Calming Activities:** What relaxation techniques will you use? (e.g., reading, brain dump, stretching)

  (Space for planning)

- **Environment Optimization:** How will you improve your sleep environment? (Cool, dark, quiet)

  (Space for planning)

Key Ideas to Note

- A successful morning for a night owl begins the night before.
- The evening routine is about using your energized evening self to support your foggy morning self.

- "Pre-Morning Prep" focuses on minimizing decisions (priorities, food, environment) to reduce friction in the morning.

- "Revenge Bedtime Procrastination" is a response to stress and lack of downtime. Combat it by scheduling intentional leisure earlier.

- The "Closing Ceremony" is a sequence of actions to wind down, minimize blue light, calm the mind, and optimize the sleep environment.

With this scaffolding erected in the evening, we can now focus on how to approach the actual process of waking up and starting the day.

Chapter 6: The Art of the Slow Start and the MVM

Most morning advice is aggressive. It's about "attacking the day," "crushing your goals," and jumping out of bed with enthusiasm.

This advice is terrible for night owls.

When you are dealing with severe sleep inertia, the last thing you need is aggression. You don't need a drill sergeant; you need a gentle nudge.

Trying to force a fast start is like trying to sprint immediately after waking up from surgery. It's painful and counterproductive.

This chapter is about embracing the Art of the Slow Start. It's about recognizing that for night owls, slow is smooth, and smooth is fast. It's about creating a morning routine that is compassionate, realistic, and effective.

The Concept of Minimum Viable Morning (MVM)

In the tech world, there is a concept called the *Minimum Viable Product (MVP)*. It's the simplest version of a product that you can launch to test your idea and gather feedback.

We can apply this concept to our mornings. We call it the *Minimum Viable Morning (MVM)*.

The MVM is the least amount of action necessary to gain momentum and transition into your day without causing stress.

The Trap of the "Perfect Morning Routine"

Many people get stuck because they try to create the "perfect morning routine." They think they need to meditate for 30 minutes, exercise for an hour, journal, read, and learn a new language—all before breakfast.

This is unrealistic and overwhelming. When you set the bar too high, you are likely to fail. And when you fail, you feel guilty and give up entirely.

The MVM is the antidote to this perfectionism. It's about lowering the bar and focusing on consistency.

What Does the MVM Look Like?

Your MVM will depend on your specific needs and circumstances. But it should be simple, short, and easy to execute even when you are tired.

Here are some examples of MVM actions:

- Drink a glass of water.
- Brush your teeth.
- Make your bed.
- Stretch for 5 minutes.
- Make coffee or tea.

That's it. If that's all you do, you have succeeded.

The Power of Small Wins

The MVM works because it creates a sense of accomplishment and momentum. When you complete a small task, your brain gets a hit of dopamine, the neurotransmitter associated with motivation.

This small win makes it easier to tackle the next task, and the next.

It's about building momentum gradually, rather than trying to generate it all at once.

The MVM on Difficult Days

The MVM is especially important on difficult days—when you are sick, stressed, or extremely tired. On these days, your goal is not to have a perfect morning. Your goal is to survive and minimize the damage.

By focusing on the bare minimum, you maintain consistency and prevent the feeling of failure that can derail your progress.

Perfectionism is the enemy of progress. Keep it simple.

How Aggressive Alarms Sabotage Night Owls

The traditional approach to waking up is jarring and stressful. It's designed to shock your system into alertness. But for night owls, this approach backfires.

The Problem with Aggressive Alarms

A loud, sudden alarm triggers a stress response in your body. It floods your system with cortisol, the stress hormone.

While this might wake you up, it also makes you feel anxious, irritable, and even more foggy. It sets a negative tone for the rest of the day.

We need to rethink the alarm clock. Instead of a shock, we need a gentle transition.

- **Wake-Up Lights:** These lights simulate a sunrise, gradually brightening your room before your alarm goes off. This allows your body to naturally stop producing melatonin and wake up more gently.
- **Gentle Sounds:** If you use an audible alarm, choose a sound that is gentle and gradually increases in volume, rather than a blaring noise.

The Snooze Button Trap

The snooze button is a symptom of a deeper problem: You are not getting enough sleep, or you are trying to wake up at the wrong time.

When you hit the snooze button, the sleep you get in between alarms is fragmented and low quality. It actually increases sleep inertia and makes you feel more tired.

The solution is to set your alarm for the time you actually need to wake up, and then stick to it. If you find it impossible to get out of bed, it means you need to adjust your sleep schedule, not rely on the snooze button.

The Sabotage of Immediate Engagement

Another common mistake is immediately jumping into work or checking your phone as soon as you wake up.

When you check your email or social media first thing in the morning, you are allowing other people's priorities to dictate your day. You are starting your day in a reactive mode, rather than a proactive mode.

Furthermore, when your brain is still in sleep inertia, you are not capable of handling complex information or stressful inputs. Trying to process emails or news headlines can trigger a stress response and derail your focus.

This immediate engagement sabotages your productivity and well-being. It reinforces the feeling of being rushed and overwhelmed.

The "Buffer Zone"

The antidote to the aggressive start is the *"Buffer Zone"*.

The Buffer Zone is an intentional space between waking up and starting your workday. It's a period of time dedicated to your well-being and mental preparation.

This is not a luxury. It's a necessity for night owls.

The Buffer Zone allows your brain to gradually boot up, reducing the impact of sleep inertia. It allows you to start your day calmly and intentionally, rather than rushing into a frenzy of activity.

How Long Should the Buffer Zone Be?

The length of the Buffer Zone will depend on your individual needs and schedule. However, a minimum of 30 minutes is recommended. Ideally, it should be 60 to 90 minutes.

If you think you don't have time for a Buffer Zone, reconsider your priorities. The time you invest in your Buffer Zone will pay dividends in increased productivity and reduced stress throughout the day.

What to Do in the Buffer Zone?

The Buffer Zone should be filled with activities that nourish your mind and body.

- **Mindfulness or Meditation:** Even 5 minutes of focused breathing can help calm your nervous system.
- **Light Reading:** Reading a physical book (not news or work-related material) can gently engage your brain.

- **Journaling:** Writing down your thoughts and intentions can help you gain clarity and focus.
- **Enjoying a Beverage:** Sipping a cup of coffee or tea mindfully can be a calming ritual.
- **Spending Time in Nature:** If possible, spend a few minutes outside.

The Non-Negotiable Rule: No Screens

The most important rule of the Buffer Zone is to avoid screens, especially phones and computers. This time is for you, not for the digital world.

Keep your phone out of the bedroom. Don't check your email until your Buffer Zone is over.

By creating this intentional space, you are taking control of your morning. You are signaling to your brain that your well-being is a priority.

The Core Trio for Clearing the Fog

While the Buffer Zone provides the space, there are specific actions you can take to accelerate the process of clearing the morning fog (sleep inertia).

We call these the *Core Trio*: Hydration, Light, and Gentle Movement.

These three elements work together to signal to your body that it's time to wake up and stabilize your energy levels.

1. Hydration

Your body is dehydrated after a night of sleep. Hydration is the first and most important step to waking up your system.

- **The Action:** Drink a large glass of water as soon as you wake up.
- **The Benefit:** It helps flush out toxins, boost your metabolism, and improve cognitive function.

Keep a glass of water by your bed so you can drink it immediately.

2. Light (At the Right Time)

Light is the most powerful signal for regulating your circadian rhythm. Getting light exposure in the morning helps stop the production of melatonin and increase alertness.

- **The Action:** Get exposure to bright light within the first hour of waking up.
- **The Benefit:** It reduces sleep inertia, improves mood, and helps regulate your sleep schedule.

Strategies for Getting Light:

- **Natural Sunlight:** The best option is to get outside and get natural sunlight for 10-15 minutes.
- **Light Therapy Lamp:** If you wake up before the sun or live in a dark climate, use a light therapy lamp (at least 10,000 lux) for 15-30 minutes.

A Note for Night Owls: While light is crucial in the morning, it's equally important to avoid bright light in the evening, as it can delay your sleep onset.

3. Gentle Movement (Not HIIT)

Movement helps increase blood flow to the brain, improving alertness and reducing stiffness.

However, intense exercise (like HIIT or heavy lifting) first thing in the morning can be counterproductive for night owls. It can spike your cortisol levels and leave you feeling exhausted.

Focus on gentle movement instead.

- **The Action:** Engage in 5-15 minutes of gentle movement.
- **The Benefit:** It improves circulation, reduces stiffness, and boosts mood without causing stress.

Examples of Gentle Movement:

- Stretching
- Yoga
- A short walk
- Tai Chi

The goal is not to break a sweat. The goal is to wake up your body.

Integrating the Core Trio

The Core Trio can be easily integrated into your MVM and Buffer Zone.

- Wake up and drink water (Hydration).
- Sit by your light therapy lamp or go for a short walk (Light and Movement).

By focusing on these three simple actions, you can significantly improve the quality of your mornings and set yourself up for a productive day.

Exercise: Building Your Slow Start Strategy

This exercise will help you implement the concepts of the Slow Start, MVM, and the Core Trio.

Step 1: Define Your Minimum Viable Morning (MVM)

List the 3-5 essential actions you need to take to gain momentum. Keep it simple.

- *Example: Drink water, brush teeth, stretch for 5 minutes, make coffee.*

(Space for planning)

Step 2: Design Your Buffer Zone

Determine how long your Buffer Zone will be and what activities you will do.

- **Duration:** (e.g., 30 minutes, 60 minutes)

  (Space for planning)

- **Activities:** (e.g., reading, meditation, enjoying coffee)

  (Space for planning)

- **The Rule:** How will you ensure you avoid screens during this time?

  (Space for planning)

Step 3: Integrate the Core Trio

How will you incorporate Hydration, Light, and Gentle Movement into your morning routine?

- **Hydration:** (e.g., Drink a glass of water immediately upon waking)

  (Space for planning)

- **Light:** (e.g., Use a light therapy lamp for 15 minutes while reading)

(Space for planning)

- **Gentle Movement:** (e.g., 10 minutes of stretching or a short walk)

(Space for planning)

Step 4: Rethink Your Alarm

How can you make your wake-up process less aggressive?

- *Example: Use a wake-up light or a gentle alarm sound.*
- *Example: Set the alarm for the actual time I need to wake up and commit to not hitting snooze.*

(Space for planning)

Key Ideas from Chapter 6

- Aggressive morning routines are counterproductive for night owls. Embrace the Art of the Slow Start.

- The Minimum Viable Morning (MVM) is the least amount of action necessary to gain momentum. Focus on small wins and consistency.

- Aggressive alarms and immediate engagement with screens sabotage your productivity and well-being.

- The "Buffer Zone" is an intentional space between waking up and starting work, dedicated to your well-being and mental preparation.

- The Core Trio (Hydration, Light, and Gentle Movement) helps clear the morning fog and stabilize your energy levels.

These building blocks enable us to move into the practical implementation of customizing a routine that fits your life and goals.

Chapter 7: The Modular Morning Method

You've probably tried to follow a strict morning routine before. You see those intricate schedules online: 5:00 AM wake up, 5:15 AM meditation, 5:45 AM workout, 6:30 AM journaling, and so on.

You try it, and maybe it works for a few days. But then life happens. You get sick, you have a late night, or you just wake up feeling exceptionally tired. The routine falls apart.

When this happens, many people feel like they have failed. They believe, "I *must* follow this routine perfectly, or it's pointless." This all-or-nothing thinking is a trap. It leads to frustration and makes you want to give up entirely.

The problem isn't you. The problem is the rigidity of the routine. Life is not rigid. Your energy levels are not rigid. A routine designed for a robot will not work for a human being, especially a night owl dealing with fluctuating energy levels.

This chapter introduces the *Modular Morning Method*. It's a flexible, realistic approach to building a morning routine that adapts to you, rather than forcing you to adapt to it.

A Flexible, "Building Block" Approach

The Modular Morning Method rejects the idea of a fixed, minute-by-minute timeline. Instead, it uses a "building block" approach.

Think of it like building with LEGOs. You have a collection of different blocks. You can assemble them in various ways depending on what you want to build that day.

In this method, the "blocks" are categories of activities that support your transition from sleep to wakefulness. You can choose which blocks to use, how long they last, and in what order to arrange them, based on the day's demands and your energy levels.

The Principles of the Modular Method

1. **Flexibility over Rigidity:** The routine serves you; you do not serve the routine.
2. **Consistency over Intensity:** It's better to do a 5-minute routine consistently than a 60-minute routine occasionally.
3. **Self-Awareness over External Rules:** You decide what you need based on how you feel, not based on what a guru tells you to do.

Why This Works for Night Owls

This approach is particularly effective for night owls because it accommodates the reality of sleep inertia and the need for a slow start.

If you wake up feeling foggy, you can choose blocks that focus on gentle activation and minimize cognitive demand. If you have an early meeting, you can shorten the blocks to fit the time available.

It removes the pressure to perform at your peak first thing in the morning. It gives you permission to warm up gradually.

The goal is not to have a perfect morning. The goal is to have a functional morning that sets you up for a successful day.

Let's look at the core customizable blocks.

The Customizable Blocks

The Modular Morning Method consists of four core blocks. You can think of these as containers you fill with activities that work for you.

Block 1: The Wake-Up Sequence

This block covers the immediate actions you take upon waking. The goal is to transition from sleep to wakefulness as gently and effectively as possible. This is where you address the physical aspects of waking up.

Key Components:

- **Alarm Strategies:** As discussed in Chapter 6, aggressive alarms are counterproductive.
  - *Options:* Use a wake-up light (simulated sunrise), gentle sounds that gradually increase in volume, or a vibration alarm.
- **The "Anti-Snooze" Tactic:** Hitting the snooze button increases sleep inertia. We need a strategy to break this habit.
  - *The Tactic:* Set your alarm for the actual time you need to wake up. Place the alarm across the room so you have to physically get out of bed. Immediately follow this with an action that makes it harder to get back into bed (e.g., going straight to the bathroom).
- **Hydration:** This is the most crucial step.
  - *Action:* Drink a large glass of water immediately. Keep it by your bed.
- **Light Exposure (Initial Dose):** Signaling to your brain that it's morning.
  - *Action:* Turn on a bright light (ideally a light therapy lamp) or open the curtains as soon as you are out of bed.

Time Allocation: 5-15 minutes.

The Mindset Shift: Instead of resisting the alarm, view the Wake-Up Sequence as the first act of self-care. You are gently guiding your body into the day.

Block 2: Gentle Activation

This block is about waking up your body and mind without causing stress. The goal is to clear the remaining sleep inertia and stabilize your energy. This is your Buffer Zone.

Remember, night owls often feel stiff and grumpy in the morning. This block is designed to address that reality.

Key Components:

- **Gentle Movement:** Focus on circulation and flexibility, not cardio.
  - ○ *Options:* Stretching, yoga, a short walk outside, or simply moving around the house while making coffee.
- **Meditation for the Grumpy:** Traditional meditation can be difficult when you are tired and irritable.
  - ○ *Options:* Focus on simple breathing exercises (e.g., 4-7-8 breathing), guided meditations, or simply sitting quietly and noticing your surroundings without judgment. If meditation feels impossible, skip it. It's not mandatory.
- **Hygiene and Grooming:** The physical act of showering, washing your face, and getting dressed can significantly improve your alertness and mood.
- **Nourishment (Optional):** Some people prefer to eat breakfast right away; others prefer to wait. Listen to your body.
  - ○ *Tip:* If you do eat, focus on protein and healthy fats to stabilize blood sugar.

Time Allocation: 15-60 minutes (depending on available time and needs).

The Mindset Shift: This is not about self-improvement; it's about self-regulation. You are giving your nervous system what it needs to function optimally.

Block 3: Mental Warm-up

This block is about gradually engaging your brain and preparing for focused work. The goal is to transition from a state of rest to a state of alertness without overwhelming your cognitive resources.

Crucially, this is **not** the time for deep work or complex decision-making. Your brain is still warming up.

Key Components:

- **Light Reading:** Engaging your mind with low-demand input.
  - *Options:* Read a physical book (fiction or non-fiction that interests you). Avoid news or social media, which can trigger stress.
- **Journaling:** Clearing your mind and setting intentions.
  - *Options:* Brain dump (writing down everything on your mind), gratitude journaling (listing three things you are grateful for), or free writing.
- **Reviewing Goals (Not Planning):** Reminding yourself of your priorities.
  - *Action:* Look at the Top 3 priorities you set the night before (in Chapter 5). Do not try to create a new plan or an elaborate to-do list.
- **Hobbies and Play:** Engaging in activities that bring you joy and creativity.
  - *Options:* Playing a musical instrument, sketching, or spending time with a pet.

Time Allocation: 15-60 minutes.

The Mindset Shift: Think of this as stretching for your brain. You wouldn't start a race without warming up your muscles. Don't start your workday without warming up your brain.

Block 4: The Launchpad

This block is the transition into your workday. The goal is to start your work calmly and intentionally, rather than rushing into a reactive mode.

Key Components:

- **Environment Setup:** Preparing your workspace.
    - *Action:* Clear any clutter from your desk, open the necessary applications on your computer, and gather the tools you need.
- **The "First Task" Strategy:** Choosing the right task to start with.
    - *Strategy:* Start with a task that is important but not overwhelming. This could be a simpler task that helps you gain momentum (a "warm-up task").
- **Time Blocking (Optional):** Allocating specific times for specific tasks.
    - *Action:* Roughly outline your schedule for the day, keeping in mind your energy levels. Schedule deep work for your peak hours (afternoon/evening).
- **The Transition Signal:** A clear action that marks the beginning of the workday.
    - *Action:* This could be opening your email, starting a timer, or putting on a specific playlist.

Time Allocation: 5-15 minutes.

The Mindset Shift: You are starting your day proactively, not reactively. You are in control of your focus and attention.

How to Assemble the Blocks

The beauty of the Modular Morning Method is its flexibility. You can assemble the blocks based on the day's demands and your energy levels.

Here are some scenarios:

Scenario 1: A Typical Workday (Ample Time)

You wake up naturally and have plenty of time before you need to start work.

- Wake-Up Sequence (10 min)
- Gentle Activation (45 min): Short walk, shower, breakfast.
- Mental Warm-up (45 min): Reading, journaling.
- Launchpad (10 min)

Total Time: 1 hour 50 minutes.

Scenario 2: An Early Meeting (Limited Time)

You have to wake up earlier than usual for a meeting. Your priority is to be functional and presentable.

- Wake-Up Sequence (10 min): Hydration, light lamp.
- Gentle Activation (30 min): Shower, get dressed, coffee. (Skip the walk).
- Mental Warm-up (10 min): Review meeting agenda and goals. (Skip reading/journaling).
- Launchpad (5 min)

Total Time: 55 minutes.

Scenario 3: A Low Energy Day (High Sleep Inertia)

You wake up feeling exhausted and foggy. Your priority is to minimize stress and gradually increase energy.

- Wake-Up Sequence (15 min): Slow transition, extra hydration.

- Gentle Activation (60 min): Long, gentle stretching, quiet time with tea.

- Mental Warm-up (30 min): Light reading (something comforting).

- Launchpad (10 min): Start with the easiest task.

Total Time: 1 hour 55 minutes.

The Key Questions to Ask Yourself Each Morning:

When you wake up, ask yourself these three questions to determine how to assemble your blocks:

1. **How much time do I have?** (Constraints)
2. **How much energy do I have?** (Capacity)
3. **What do I need most right now?** (Priorities)

By answering these questions honestly and without judgment, you can create a morning routine that supports you exactly where you are.

Stop trying to force yourself into a routine that doesn't fit. Start building a routine that adapts to your life.

Exercise: Building Your Modular Morning Menu

This exercise will help you brainstorm activities for each block and create your personalized Modular Morning Menu.

Step 1: Brainstorm Activities

For each block, list the activities that appeal to you. Be realistic about what you are likely to do.

- **Block 1: Wake-Up Sequence (5-15 min)**
  - *Examples: Wake-up light, hydration, open curtains.*

(Space for brainstorming)

- **Block 2: Gentle Activation (15-60 min)**
  - *Examples: Stretching, short walk, shower, breakfast, meditation.*

(Space for brainstorming)

- **Block 3: Mental Warm-up (15-60 min)**
  - *Examples: Reading, journaling, reviewing goals, playing music.*

(Space for brainstorming)

- **Block 4: The Launchpad (5-15 min)**
  - *Examples: Tidy desk, start warm-up task, time blocking.*

(Space for brainstorming)

Step 2: Identify Your Non-Negotiables

Look at your list. Which 2-3 activities are most important for your well-being and productivity? These are your non-negotiables.

- *Example: Hydration, light exposure, reviewing goals.*

(Space for reflection)

Step 3: Practice Assembly

Imagine you have a busy day tomorrow with only 45 minutes for your morning routine. How would you assemble your blocks using your menu?

(Space for planning)

Imagine you have a slow day tomorrow with 2 hours for your morning routine. How would you assemble your blocks?

(Space for planning)

Key Ideas from Chapter 7

- Rigid, minute-by-minute routines often fail because they don't account for the reality of life and fluctuating energy levels.

- The Modular Morning Method uses a flexible, "building block" approach that adapts to your needs.

- The four customizable blocks are: The Wake-Up Sequence, Gentle Activation, Mental Warm-up, and The Launchpad.

- Each block focuses on a specific aspect of the transition from sleep to wakefulness.

- You can assemble the blocks based on how much time and energy you have, and what your priorities are for the day.

- Flexibility and self-awareness are more important than perfection and rigidity.

With these tools in your toolkit, we can now look at how these blocks come together in real-life scenarios for different types of night owls.

Chapter 8: Anti-5AM Routine Templates

The Modular Morning Method provides the framework. But what does it look like in practice?

It's easy to get overwhelmed by the possibilities. Sometimes, you just need a starting point—a template you can adapt to your own life.

This chapter provides four templates for different types of night owls. These are not prescriptions. They are examples designed to inspire you and show you how the principles of the Anti-5AM can be applied in various situations.

Remember the core philosophy: These routines prioritize energy management, the slow start, and working with your biology, not against it. They are designed to help you wake up well, regardless of the time on the clock.

Template 1: The "9 AM Corporate Warrior"

This template is for night owls who have to conform to a traditional 9-to-5 schedule. The challenge here is the conflict between your biological clock and your social clock. You have to wake up early, even though your body resists it.

The Constraints: Early wake-up time (e.g., 7 AM), limited time in the morning, need to be professional and functional early.

The Strategy: The "Decoy Morning"

The key strategy here is the "Decoy Morning." This means using the morning hours for low-demand tasks and saving your cognitive resources for the afternoon, when your energy peaks.

The Routine (Wake-up at 7:00 AM, Start Work at 9:00 AM)

Evening Prep (Crucial):

- Prepare everything the night before: outfit, lunch, coffee maker.
- Identify Top 3 priorities, focusing on tasks that can be done in the afternoon.
- Closing Ceremony: Wind down early, optimize sleep environment.

Block 1: Wake-Up Sequence (7:00 - 7:15 AM)

- 7:00 AM: Wake up with a wake-up light (starts brightening at 6:30 AM). Gentle alarm sound.
- Hydration: Drink a large glass of water.
- Light Exposure: Turn on a light therapy lamp while getting ready.

Block 2: Gentle Activation (7:15 - 8:00 AM)

- Movement: 10 minutes of gentle stretching or yoga to reduce stiffness.
- Hygiene: Shower, get dressed (pre-selected outfit).
- Nourishment: Simple breakfast (protein-focused, pre-prepared).

Block 3: Mental Warm-up (8:00 - 8:45 AM)

- Commute Strategy: Use the commute for a mental warm-up, not stress.
  - Listen to a podcast or audiobook (engaging but not demanding).
  - Avoid checking email or news.
- If working from home: 15 minutes of light reading or reviewing goals.

Block 4: The Launchpad (8:45 - 9:00 AM)

- Environment Setup: Organize desk, get coffee.
- Review Priorities: Look at the Top 3 list.

The Workday Strategy (Energy Management):

- **Morning (9 AM - 12 PM):** Focus on low-demand tasks: emails, administrative work, routine meetings. This is the "Decoy Morning."
- **Afternoon (1 PM - 5 PM):** Focus on high-demand tasks: deep work, complex problem-solving, important decisions. This is your Peak.

The Mindset Shift: Accept that you won't be at your best in the morning. Your goal is to survive the morning and thrive in the afternoon.

Template 2: The "11 AM Creative/Freelancer"

This template is for night owls who have full control over their schedule. The challenge here is the lack of structure and the potential for guilt about waking up late.

The goal is to embrace your natural rhythm, maximize your creativity, and create a structure that supports your well-being.

The Constraints: Flexible schedule, potential for distraction, need for self-discipline.

The Strategy: The Intentional Slow Start

The key strategy here is to fully embrace the slow start and use the morning for inspiration and alignment.

The Routine (Wake-up at 10:00 AM, Start Work at 12:00 PM)

Evening Prep:

- Identify Top 3 creative priorities for the next day.
- Tidy workspace to create a calm environment.
- Embrace late-night creativity if it strikes, but ensure adequate sleep.

Block 1: Wake-Up Sequence (10:00 - 10:15 AM)

- 10:00 AM: Wake up naturally (no alarm if possible) or with a gentle alarm.
- Hydration: Drink water.
- Light Exposure: Open curtains, let the natural light in.

Block 2: Gentle Activation (10:15 - 11:00 AM)

- Movement: A mindful walk outside (combining movement and light).
- Hygiene: Shower, grooming.
- Nourishment: A nourishing breakfast, enjoyed mindfully (not at the desk).

Block 3: Mental Warm-up (11:00 AM - 11:45 AM)

- Inspiration: Engage with content that sparks creativity.
  - Read a book related to your field.
  - Journaling or free writing.

- Meditation: 10 minutes of mindfulness to clear the mind.

Block 4: The Launchpad (11:45 AM - 12:00 PM)

- Environment Setup: Prepare creative tools.
- Review Priorities: Look at the Top 3 creative tasks.
- Transition Signal: Start a focused work playlist.

The Workday Strategy (Energy Management):

- **Late Morning/Early Afternoon (12 PM - 3 PM):** Ramp-up period. Focus on moderate-demand tasks: emails, planning, research.
- **Late Afternoon/Evening (3 PM - 7 PM):** Peak period. Focus on deep creative work, flow state.
- **Late Evening (9 PM onwards):** Second wind (optional). Focus on brainstorming, experimentation, or relaxation.

The Mindset Shift: Reject the guilt about waking up late. Recognize that your schedule is optimized for your creativity and productivity.

Template 3: The "Hectic Household"

This template is for night owls who have responsibilities for others (children, family members). The challenge here is the unpredictability and the demands of others, which often conflict with your need for a slow start.

The goal is to create pockets of calm amidst the chaos, prioritize your well-being, and manage your energy sustainably.

The Constraints: External demands, interruptions, limited time for self-care, early start (if children have school).

The Strategy: The Anchor Routine

The key strategy here is the "Anchor Routine." This means having a few non-negotiable actions that ground you, even when everything else is unpredictable.

The Routine (Wake-up at 7:30 AM, Household Active until 9:00 AM)

Evening Prep (Essential for Survival):

- Prepare everything for the household: children's clothes, lunches, backpacks.
- Minimize decisions for yourself: outfit, breakfast.
- Communicate your needs to your partner (if applicable): e.g., "I need 10 minutes of quiet time in the morning."

Block 1: Wake-Up Sequence (7:30 - 7:45 AM)

- Wake up slightly before the household (even 15 minutes helps).
- Hydration and Light.
- Anchor Action 1: 5 minutes of quiet breathing or stretching before the chaos begins.

Block 2: Gentle Activation (The "Managed Chaos" Phase) (7:45 - 8:30 AM)

- Focus on essential tasks: getting children ready, breakfast.
- Minimize engagement in stressful conversations.
- Practice mindfulness amidst the chaos: notice your breath, stay present.

Block 3: Mental Warm-up (The "Transition Buffer") (8:30 - 9:00 AM)

- After the household transitions (e.g., children leave for school), create a buffer zone.

- Anchor Action 2: 15 minutes of intentional downtime.
    - Sit down and enjoy a cup of coffee or tea.
    - Light reading or listening to calming music.
    - Do not jump straight into chores or work.

Block 4: The Launchpad (9:00 - 9:15 AM)

- Transition into your workday or responsibilities.
- Review Priorities: Focus on the most important tasks.

The Workday Strategy (Energy Management):

- **Prioritize Rest:** Take advantage of any opportunity to rest or recharge during the day.
- **Align Tasks with Energy:** Schedule demanding tasks for the afternoon/evening when your energy is higher.
- **Set Boundaries:** Communicate your boundaries and protect your downtime.

The Mindset Shift: Reject the pressure to be a "perfect parent/caregiver" (especially the cheerful morning person stereotype). Focus on being present and compassionate, both to yourself and your family.

Template 4: The "Bare Minimum"

This template is for the days when everything goes wrong. You are sick, stressed, extremely tired, or dealing with a crisis. The challenge here is the overwhelming feeling of exhaustion and the tendency to give up entirely.

The goal is to survive the day, minimize the damage, and maintain consistency with the bare minimum effort. This is the Minimum Viable Morning (MVM) in action.

The Constraints: Very low energy, high stress, limited capacity.

The Strategy: Radical Self-Compassion

The key strategy here is radical self-compassion. Reject the urge to criticize yourself or force productivity.

The Routine (Wake-up Time: Whenever Necessary)

Evening Prep (If possible):

- If you anticipate a difficult day, lower your expectations in advance.
- Communicate your needs to others (e.g., cancel plans, ask for help).

Block 1: Wake-Up Sequence (5 minutes)

- Get out of bed (this is the main goal).
- Hydration.

Block 2: Gentle Activation (15-30 minutes)

- Basic hygiene: Wash face, brush teeth.
- Change clothes (even if it's just clean pajamas).
- Eat something simple (e.g., toast, fruit).

Block 3: Mental Warm-up (5 minutes)

- Acknowledge your feelings without judgment.
- Identify one essential task for the day (e.g., attend a crucial meeting, eat lunch).

Block 4: The Launchpad (1 minute)

- Transition into the essential task.

The Workday Strategy (Energy Management):

- **Cancel/Delegate:** Cancel non-essential tasks and meetings. Delegate responsibilities if possible.
- **Focus on Survival:** Prioritize rest, hydration, and nourishment.
- **Low-Demand Tasks:** If you must work, focus on the easiest, lowest-demand tasks.

The Mindset Shift: This is not a failure. This is a strategic retreat. By honoring your needs on difficult days, you are building resilience and preventing burnout.

Remember: Consistency is not about being perfect every day. It's about showing up and doing what you can with what you have.

These templates are starting points. Take what works for you, discard what doesn't, and create a routine that honors your biology and supports your goals.

Exercise: Adapting the Templates

This exercise will help you adapt the templates to your specific lifestyle and needs.

Step 1: Choose Your Primary Template

Which template resonates most with your current situation?

- Corporate Warrior (Fixed Schedule)
- Creative/Freelancer (Flexible Schedule)
- Hectic Household (Parents/Caregivers)
- Bare Minimum (Crisis Days)

(Space for selection)

Step 2: Customize the Blocks

Review the chosen template and customize the activities in each block based on your preferences and constraints. Use your Modular Morning Menu from Chapter 7.

- **Evening Prep:**

  (Space for customization)

- **Block 1: Wake-Up Sequence:**

  (Space for customization)

- **Block 2: Gentle Activation:**

  (Space for customization)

- **Block 3: Mental Warm-up:**

  (Space for customization)

- **Block 4: The Launchpad:**

  (Space for customization)

Step 3: Define Your Workday Strategy

How will you apply the principles of energy management throughout your day?

- **Trough (Low Energy):** What tasks will you focus on?

  (Space for planning)

- **Peak (High Energy):** How will you protect this time for deep work?

  (Space for planning)

Step 4: Reflect on the Mindset Shift

What irrational beliefs or pressures do you need to reject to make this routine work for you?

- *Example: The belief that I must be highly productive in the morning.*

(Space for reflection)

Key Ideas from Chapter 8

- Templates provide a starting point for implementing the Modular Morning Method in different life scenarios.
- The "Corporate Warrior" template focuses on the "Decoy Morning" strategy to manage the conflict between biology and schedule.
- The "Creative/Freelancer" template emphasizes the intentional slow start and maximizing creativity.
- The "Hectic Household" template uses "Anchor Routines" to create pockets of calm amidst the chaos.
- The "Bare Minimum" template focuses on radical self-compassion and survival on difficult days.
- The key is to adapt the templates to your specific needs and prioritize energy management throughout the day.

Having mapped this terrain of personalized routines, we now need to address the reality of living as a night owl in a world designed for early birds.

"Chapter 9: Thriving in the 9-to-5 World

It's one thing to understand your biology. It's another thing to explain it to your boss who has scheduled a mandatory brainstorming session at 8:00 AM.

The reality is that the world, particularly the corporate world, is built for morning people. The 9-to-5 schedule (which often feels more like 8-to-6) directly conflicts with the natural rhythm of a night owl.

This conflict creates stress. You might feel like you are constantly swimming upstream. You might worry that your colleagues perceive you as less committed because you are not chipper and energized first thing in the morning.

You might believe, "I *must* adapt to this schedule to keep my job," or "If I can't perform well in the morning, I am a failure."

These beliefs are understandable, but they are not entirely rational. You cannot change your biology. But you *can* change how you navigate the environment.

This chapter is about practical strategies for surviving and thriving in a 9-to-5 culture. It's about managing your energy, communicating your needs, and challenging the outdated assumptions that govern the workplace.

Surviving Early Meeting Hell

Early meetings are the bane of a night owl's existence. You are expected to be alert, engaged, and make important decisions when your brain is still in sleep inertia.

It's not ideal. But it's often unavoidable. Here's how to survive them without sabotaging your day.

1. Preparation is Everything (The Night Before)

If you have an early meeting, your preparation the night before is crucial.

- **Information Prep:** Review the agenda and materials the night before, when your brain is sharp. Write down your key points and questions.
- **Decision Prep:** If possible, make any necessary decisions in advance. Don't leave complex thinking for the morning.
- **Logistics Prep:** Eliminate all logistical friction. Choose your outfit, pack your bag, prepare your breakfast.

2. Optimize Your Wake-Up Sequence

On early start days, your Wake-Up Sequence is critical.

- **Light is Your Ally:** Use a light therapy lamp as soon as you wake up to help clear the fog.
- **Movement (Gentle):** A short burst of gentle movement (stretching, walking) can help increase alertness.
- **Caffeine (Strategic Use):** Caffeine can help boost alertness, but use it strategically. Don't overdo it, as it can increase anxiety.

3. Managing Engagement During the Meeting

During the meeting, your goal is to remain engaged without exhausting your cognitive resources.

- **Active Listening:** Focus on listening actively. Take notes, ask clarifying questions.
- **Contribute Strategically:** Rely on the preparation you did the night before. Present your points clearly and concisely.

- **Delay Complex Decisions:** If possible, avoid making major decisions during the meeting. Say, "That's an important point. I want to give it careful consideration and will follow up this afternoon."

4. The Post-Meeting Recovery

After the meeting, you need a brief recovery period.

- **Take a Break:** Even a 5-minute break can help reset your nervous system.
- **Hydrate and Nourish:** Drink water and have a healthy snack to stabilize your energy.
- **Don't Jump into Deep Work:** Transition into low-demand tasks first.

Challenging the Catastrophe Mindset

It's easy to "awfulize" early meetings. You might think, "This is unbearable. I can't handle this."

But it is bearable. You can handle it. It's uncomfortable, but it's not a catastrophe.

When you accept the discomfort without resisting it, you reduce the associated stress and anxiety.

Handling Low-Resistance Tasks

In Chapter 3, we introduced the concept of energy management: aligning tasks with your energy levels. For night owls in a 9-to-5 job, this means recognizing that the morning is your cognitive low point.

The *"Decoy Morning"* strategy is about using this time strategically. It's about appearing productive while conserving your brainpower for your peak hours.

What Are Low-Resistance Tasks?

Low-resistance tasks are activities that require minimal cognitive effort, creativity, or decision-making. They are the tasks you can do almost on autopilot.

- **Administrative Tasks:** Organizing files, cleaning your inbox, submitting expenses.
- **Routine Communication:** Responding to simple emails, checking notifications.
- **Planning and Organizing:** Reviewing your schedule, tidying your workspace.
- **Learning (Passive):** Watching training videos, reading industry news.

The Implementation Strategy

1. **Identify Your Tasks:** At the beginning of the week (or the night before), identify all the low-resistance tasks you need to complete.
2. **Schedule Them for the Morning:** Block out your mornings for these tasks.
3. **Protect Your Afternoon:** Block out your afternoons for high-resistance tasks (deep work, complex problem-solving, creativity).

The Benefits of the Decoy Morning

- **Conserves Energy:** You save your valuable cognitive resources for when you need them most.
- **Reduces Stress:** You avoid the frustration of trying to do deep work when your brain is foggy.
- **Creates Momentum:** You build a sense of accomplishment by completing tasks, even if they are simple.
- **Manages Perception:** You appear busy and engaged to your colleagues and managers.

A Case Example

Consider a marketing manager who used to try to write creative copy in the morning. They struggled and felt frustrated. When they implemented the Decoy Morning strategy, they shifted their schedule.

They used the morning for responding to emails, analyzing data reports, and attending routine meetings. They reserved the afternoon for writing copy and developing strategies.

The result? Their productivity increased, their stress decreased, and the quality of their work improved.

The key is to reject the irrational belief that you *must* do your most important work first thing in the morning.

Boundaries and"Slacking Off"

One of the biggest challenges for night owls in the workplace is the perception that they are "slacking off" if they are not highly energized in the morning, or if they choose to work later in the evening.

This perception is based on the outdated assumption that productivity is tied to the clock, rather than the output.

Managing this perception requires a combination of clear communication, consistent results, and firm boundaries.

1. Focus on Results, Not Hours

The most effective way to combat the perception of slacking off is to consistently deliver high-quality results.

When your work speaks for itself, the time you start your day becomes less relevant.

- **Track Your Accomplishments:** Keep a record of your achievements and contributions.

- **Communicate Your Progress:** Make sure your manager and colleagues are aware of what you are working on and what you have accomplished.

2. Communicate Your Rhythm (Carefully)

You don't necessarily need to announce that you are a night owl. But you can communicate your energy patterns and work preferences.

- **Be Proactive:** Say, "I do my best focused work in the afternoon. I will block out that time for the project."
- **Be Clear about Availability:** If you work later in the evening, make sure your colleagues know when they can expect a response from you.

3. Set Boundaries Around Your Peak Hours

Protecting your peak hours (afternoon/evening) is crucial for your productivity and well-being.

- **Block Your Calendar:** Block out time for deep work on your calendar.
- **Minimize Interruptions:** Use status messages (e.g., "Focusing on a project"), turn off notifications, and wear headphones.
- **Say No (Respectfully):** Decline non-essential meetings or requests that interfere with your peak hours.

Challenging the Fear of Judgment

It's natural to worry about what others think. You might believe, "If my colleagues think I'm lazy, it would be terrible."

But you cannot control what others think. You can only control your actions and your responses.

If you are delivering results and meeting your responsibilities, then the judgment of others is irrelevant. Focus on your own standards, not the perceived standards of others.

Your worth is not determined by how cheerful you are at 8 AM.

Negotiating Flexible Hours (When Possible)

The ideal solution for night owls is a flexible schedule that aligns with their chronotype. While this is not always possible, the rise of remote work and the increasing focus on employee well-being have made it more feasible than ever before.

Negotiating flexible hours requires a strategic approach.

1. Build Your Case (Focus on the Benefits for the Employer)

When you approach your manager, focus on how a flexible schedule will benefit the company, not just you.

- **Increased Productivity:** Explain how working during your peak hours will allow you to produce higher quality work.
- **Improved Engagement:** Highlight how a flexible schedule will improve your morale and commitment.
- **Expanded Coverage:** If you work later, you can provide coverage for clients or colleagues in different time zones.

2. Present a Clear Proposal

Don't just ask for "flexibility." Present a clear, specific proposal.

- **Proposed Schedule:** Suggest a specific schedule (e.g., 10 AM to 6 PM, or 11 AM to 7 PM).
- **Core Hours:** Identify "core hours" when you will be available for meetings and collaboration (e.g., 12 PM to 4 PM).
- **Communication Plan:** Explain how you will stay connected with your team.

3. Suggest a Trial Period

If your manager is hesitant, suggest a trial period (e.g., 3 months). This reduces the risk for the employer and gives you an opportunity to demonstrate the effectiveness of the arrangement.

4. Be Prepared for Resistance

Your manager might resist your proposal. They might have concerns about fairness, collaboration, or productivity.

- **Listen to Their Concerns:** Acknowledge their concerns and address them directly.
- **Provide Evidence:** Share research on chronotypes and productivity (if appropriate for your workplace culture).
- **Be Flexible (Within Reason):** Be willing to compromise and find a solution that works for both you and the company.

If Negotiation Fails

If negotiation fails, don't despair. You can still use the strategies in this chapter to manage your energy and thrive within the constraints of your current situation.

And remember, the workplace is changing. If your current job is unwilling to accommodate your needs, there might be other opportunities out there that are a better fit for your biology.

Exercise: Developing Your 9-to-5 Survival Strategy

This exercise will help you create a personalized strategy for navigating your workplace as a night owl.

Step 1: Analyze Your Constraints

- What are the mandatory early starts or meetings you have to attend?

  (Space for reflection)

- How can you optimize your preparation (the night before) and recovery (afterwards) for these events?

  (Space for planning)

Step 2: Design Your Decoy Morning

- List the low-resistance tasks you can shift to your morning hours.

  (Space for brainstorming)

- How will you protect your afternoon peak hours for high-resistance tasks?

  (Space for planning)

Step 3: Manage Perception and Boundaries

- How will you communicate your work preferences and energy patterns to your colleagues and manager?

  (Space for planning)

- What boundaries do you need to set to protect your peak hours and well-being?

  (Space for planning)

Step 4: Plan for Flexibility (Optional)

- If you want to negotiate flexible hours, what is your proposed schedule?

(Space for planning)

- How will you present the benefits to your employer?

(Space for planning)

Key Ideas from Chapter 9

- The 9-to-5 culture often conflicts with the natural rhythm of night owls, but you can navigate this conflict strategically.
- Survive mandatory early starts through rigorous preparation, optimized wake-up sequences, and strategic engagement.
- The "Decoy Morning" strategy involves handling low-resistance tasks in the morning to save brainpower for peak hours.
- Manage the perception of "slacking off" by focusing on results, communicating clearly, and setting firm boundaries.
- Challenge the irrational beliefs and fears of judgment that hold you back.
- Negotiate flexible hours by focusing on the benefits for the employer and presenting a clear proposal.

This framework gives us leverage to address the challenges we face in our personal lives, where different rhythms often collide.

Chapter 10: Relationships, Family, and Flexibility

We don't live in isolation. Our sleep schedules and energy patterns affect the people around us—our partners, families, and friends.

If you are a night owl, you might feel like your rhythm is a source of conflict or misunderstanding in your relationships. You might struggle to balance your need for sleep with your desire for connection.

You might believe, "I *should* be able to adapt my schedule for others," or "If I don't conform to their expectations, they will reject me."

These beliefs create guilt and resentment. They turn a biological difference into an emotional battleground.

This chapter is about navigating the complexities of relationships as a night owl. It's about communicating your needs, finding compromises, and creating a life that honors both your biology and your connections with others.

Aligning Different Chronotypes Within a Household

The most common challenge is living with someone who has a different chronotype, especially a morning Lark.

The Lark wakes up early, energized and ready to engage. The Owl wakes up later, foggy and needing space. The Lark goes to bed early, just when the Owl is hitting their stride.

This mismatch can lead to conflict, resentment, and loneliness.

The Common Conflicts

- **The Morning Clash:** The Lark tries to engage the Owl in conversation or activity in the morning, leading to irritability and frustration.
- **The Evening Disconnect:** The Owl tries to connect with the Lark in the evening, but the Lark is tired and ready for bed.
- **The Division of Labor:** The Lark might feel like they are doing more in the morning, while the Owl might feel like they are doing more in the evening.
- **The Sleep Struggle:** Different sleep schedules can disrupt each other's sleep (e.g., alarms, noise, light).

The Solution: Communication, Compassion, and Compromise

The key to aligning different chronotypes is not to try to change each other, but to understand and respect each other's needs.

1. Understand the Biology (It's Not Personal)

The first step is to recognize that your partner's rhythm is biological, not a choice. The Lark is not trying to annoy you in the morning. The Owl is not trying to avoid you in the evening.

When you depersonalize the conflict, you can approach it with compassion and understanding.

2. Communicate Your Needs (Clearly and Calmly)

You need to communicate your needs clearly and calmly, without blame or judgment.

- **The Owl says:** "I know you are energized in the morning, but my brain doesn't function well then. I need quiet time for the first hour after I wake up. It's not that I don't want to talk to you; it's that I can't."

- **The Lark says:** "I know you are energized in the evening, but my body shuts down after 10 PM. I need to go to bed early to feel rested. It's not that I don't want to spend time with you; it's that I can't."

3. Find the "Overlap Zone"

Instead of focusing on the times when you are out of sync, focus on the times when you overlap.

- **The Afternoon/Early Evening:** This is usually the best time for connection, conversation, and shared activities.
- **Weekends:** Weekends offer more flexibility to align your schedules and spend quality time together.

4. Create Rituals of Connection

Create rituals that foster connection within the constraints of your rhythms.

- **Lunch Dates:** If possible, meet for lunch during the workday.
- **Evening Tea:** A brief connection in the evening before the Lark goes to bed.
- **Weekend Mornings (Compromise):** The Owl wakes up a bit earlier, or the Lark sleeps in a bit later, to share a relaxed morning together.

5. Practical Compromises

- **Sleep Environment:** Use separate blankets, eye masks, earplugs, or even separate bedrooms if necessary to protect each other's sleep.
- **Alarms:** Use gentle alarms (vibration, wake-up lights) to minimize disruption.
- **Division of Labor:** Divide household tasks based on energy levels, not time of day. The Lark handles the morning shift; the Owl handles the evening shift.

When you approach the challenge with collaboration rather than conflict, you can find solutions that work for both of you.

Protecting Your Sleep Schedule While Maintaining a Social Life

Another challenge for night owls is balancing their sleep schedule with their social life. Social events often happen in the evening, which can interfere with your wind-down routine and delay your bedtime.

If you have a fixed work schedule, this can lead to sleep deprivation and social jetlag.

The Irrational Belief: "I Must Say Yes to Everything"

Many people struggle with the belief that they *must* say yes to every social invitation to maintain their friendships or avoid missing out (FOMO).

This belief leads to overcommitment and exhaustion.

You need to challenge this belief and recognize that your sleep is a non-negotiable biological need.

Strategies for Balancing Sleep and Social Life

1. Prioritize and Choose Wisely

You don't have to attend every event. Prioritize the events and relationships that are most important to you.

- **Quality over Quantity:** Focus on quality interactions, rather than maximizing the number of events.
- **Say No (Gracefully):** It's okay to decline invitations. Say, "I would love to, but I have a commitment," or simply, "I can't make it this time."

2. Schedule Social Events Strategically

When possible, schedule social events at times that align better with your rhythm.

- **Weekend Afternoons:** Suggest brunches, lunches, or afternoon activities instead of late dinners.
- **Early Evenings:** If you go out on a weeknight, try to meet earlier in the evening and set a firm time to leave.

3. Communicate Your Boundaries

Let your friends and family know about your schedule and your need for sleep.

- **Be Honest:** Say, "I need to head home by 10 PM to get enough sleep before work."
- **Be Consistent:** When you respect your own boundaries, others will learn to respect them too.

4. Manage the Trade-Offs (The Sleep Budget)

Sometimes, you will choose to stay up late for a special occasion. This is fine, as long as you do it intentionally and plan for the consequences.

- **The Sleep Budget:** Think of your sleep as a budget. If you borrow from it one night, you need to pay it back.
- **Plan for Recovery:** If you stay up late, plan for a recovery period the next day. Sleep in if possible, or take a short nap.

5. Redefine "Social Life"

Social connection doesn't always have to involve late nights and high-energy activities.

- **Low-Key Evenings:** Invite friends over for a relaxed evening at home.

- **One-on-One Connections:** Focus on meaningful conversations with close friends.
- **Online Connections:** Use technology to connect with friends when your schedules don't align.

By being intentional about your social life, you can maintain your connections without sacrificing your well-being.

How to Reset Your Routine Without Guilt

We have talked a lot about creating routines and optimizing your schedule. But life is unpredictable. Things will happen that disrupt your routine.

You might get sick, have a family emergency, travel across time zones, or simply have a few late nights in a row.

When this happens, it's easy to fall into the trap of all-or-nothing thinking. You might believe, "I've ruined everything. I might as well give up."

This belief is irrational and destructive. It turns a temporary setback into a permanent failure.

The key to long-term success is not perfection. It's resilience. It's the ability to adapt to disruptions and reset your routine without guilt.

The Principles of the Routine Reset

1. Radical Acceptance (It Is What It Is)

The first step is to accept the reality of the disruption without judgment. Stop blaming yourself or "awfulizing" the situation.

You are not a failure because you got sick or stayed up late. You are a human being living a complex life.

2. Focus on the Bare Minimum (The MVM)

When you are disrupted, don't try to jump back into your full routine immediately. Focus on the Bare Minimum (the Minimum Viable Morning from Chapter 6).

- **The Essentials:** Hydration, nourishment, light, gentle movement.
- **The Non-Negotiables:** Identify the few essential tasks you need to complete.

3. Gradual Re-entry (The Ramp-Up)

Gradually ramp up your routine over a few days. Don't expect to be back at 100% immediately.

- **Day 1:** Focus on the Bare Minimum.
- **Day 2:** Add one element of your Gentle Activation block.
- **Day 3:** Add one element of your Mental Warm-up block.

4. The Power of the Evening Routine

The evening routine is your most powerful tool for resetting your rhythm.

- **The Closing Ceremony:** Focus on winding down, optimizing your sleep environment, and signaling to your body that it's time to rest.
- **Consistency is Key:** Try to maintain a consistent bedtime, even if your wake-up time is disrupted.

5. Reject the Guilt (The Most Important Step)

Guilt is the enemy of resilience. It drains your energy and makes it harder to get back on track.

When you feel guilty, challenge the underlying beliefs.

- **Irrational Belief:** "I *should* have maintained my routine perfectly."
- **Rational Belief:** "I prefer to maintain my routine, but life happens. I can handle this disruption and get back on track."

Resilience is not about never falling down. It's about getting back up, again and again, without drama or self-criticism.

Exercise: Building Your Relationship and Resilience Plan

This exercise will help you develop a personalized strategy for navigating your relationships and managing disruptions.

Step 1: Aligning Chronotypes (If applicable)

If you live with someone who has a different chronotype:

- What are the main conflicts or misunderstandings that arise from your different rhythms?

  (Space for reflection)

- How can you communicate your needs more clearly and compassionately?

  (Space for planning)

- What practical compromises can you make to respect each other's needs (e.g., sleep environment, division of labor, overlap zone)?

  (Space for planning)

Step 2: Balancing Sleep and Social Life

- What irrational beliefs do you hold about socializing and saying yes to invitations?

  (Space for reflection)

- How can you prioritize your sleep while maintaining your connections (e.g., strategic scheduling, communication, redefining social life)?

  (Space for planning)

Step 3: Planning for the Routine Reset

Think about a recent disruption to your routine.

- How did you respond? Did you fall into the trap of all-or-nothing thinking or guilt?

  (Space for reflection)

- How can you apply the principles of the Routine Reset next time a disruption occurs (Acceptance, Bare Minimum, Gradual Re-entry, Evening Routine, Rejecting Guilt)?

  (Space for planning)

Key Ideas to Note

- Navigating relationships as a night owl requires communication, compassion, and compromise.
- Align different chronotypes within a household by understanding the biology, communicating needs, finding the overlap zone, and making practical compromises.

- Protect your sleep schedule while maintaining a social life by prioritizing, scheduling strategically, communicating boundaries, and managing trade-offs.

- Challenge the irrational beliefs that lead to guilt and resentment in your relationships.

- When life happens, reset your routine without guilt by practicing radical acceptance, focusing on the bare minimum, gradually re-entering, and prioritizing your evening routine.

- Resilience, not perfection, is the key to long-term success.

As this understanding settles, we can bring together the core principles of the Anti-5AM and look at the path ahead.

Conclusion: Success After Sunrise

We began this journey with the sound of the alarm clock—that jarring noise that symbolized the tyranny of the early morning and the guilt of the night owl.

We have traveled a long way since then.

We have dismantled the myths that kept us feeling lazy, disorganized, and inadequate. We have explored the biology that shapes our rhythms and the strengths that come with being wired differently. We have developed practical strategies for optimizing our energy, reclaiming our mornings, and navigating a world that favors the early bird.

The message of this book is simple: You are not broken. You do not need to be fixed.

You are a night owl. And that is not a liability. It is a strength.

Recap of the Core Anti-5AM Principles

The Anti-5AM is more than just a collection of strategies. It's a mindset shift. It's a commitment to living life on your own terms, guided by the following principles:

1. **Biology over Bravado:** We respect our chronotype and reject the toxic productivity culture that glorifies suffering and sleep deprivation. We know that we cannot shame ourselves into becoming morning people.
2. **Energy over Hours:** We focus on managing our energy, not just our time. We align our tasks with our energy levels and optimize our peak performance windows, regardless of the clock.

3. **The Slow Start is the Fast Track:** We embrace the art of the slow start. We know that for night owls, slow is smooth, and smooth is fast. We prioritize the Buffer Zone and the Minimum Viable Morning.
4. **The Evening is the Launchpad:** We recognize that a successful morning begins the night before. We prioritize the Pre-Morning Prep and the Closing Ceremony.
5. **Flexibility over Rigidity:** We use the Modular Morning Method to create routines that adapt to our lives, rather than forcing ourselves into rigid molds. We prioritize resilience over perfection.
6. **Self-Acceptance over Self-Criticism:** We reject the guilt and shame associated with our natural rhythm. We challenge the irrational beliefs that connect early rising with virtue and success.

Natural Rhythm as Your Greatest Competitive Advantage

For too long, you have seen your night owl nature as a weakness. You have wasted energy trying to conform to a standard that was not designed for you.

It's time to flip the script.

Your natural rhythm is your greatest competitive advantage.

When you work with your biology, you unlock a level of creativity, focus, and stamina that early birds often lack. You tap into the unique strengths of the night owl: the deep thinking, the out-of-the-box solutions, the ability to thrive in the quiet hours.

In a world that is increasingly demanding creativity and complex problem-solving, these strengths are more valuable than ever.

The Knowledge Economy doesn't care when you work. It cares what you produce.

When you embrace your rhythm, you stop apologizing for who you are. You start leveraging your strengths. You stop fighting yourself and start winning.

Burn Your 5 AM Alarm Clock and Own Your Schedule

This book has provided you with the tools and the framework. But the real work begins now.

The temptation to slip back into old habits and beliefs will be strong. The pressure to conform to the 5AM culture will remain.

You have a choice to make.

You can continue to live under the tyranny of the alarm clock, feeling exhausted and frustrated.

Or you can choose to own your schedule, honor your biology, and create a life that works for you.

Burn your 5 AM alarm clock (metaphorically, or literally if you want).

Reject the guilt. Embrace the slow start. Protect your peak.

It's time to achieve success after sunrise, on your own terms.

Appendices

Appendix A: Checklist for the Perfect Evening Routine

This checklist will help you implement the strategies from Chapter 5 and create a consistent evening routine that sets you up for morning success.

Phase 1: Pre-Morning Prep (15-30 minutes before winding down)

- [ ] Identified Top 3 priorities for tomorrow.
- [ ] Wrote down the priorities and placed them where visible.
- [ ] Prepared breakfast (ingredients ready, coffee maker set).
- [ ] Packed lunch.
- [ ] Tidied workspace (cleared desk, organized tools).
- [ ] Tidied living area (quick clutter clear).
- [ ] Packed bag for tomorrow (if commuting).
- [ ] Selected outfit for tomorrow (down to the socks).

Phase 2: The Closing Ceremony (60 minutes before bed)

- [ ] Digital Sunset: Turned off all screens (phone, computer, TV).
- [ ] Brain Dump: Wrote down any lingering thoughts, worries, or ideas.
- [ ] Calming Activity: Engaged in a relaxing activity (reading a physical book, light stretching, meditation, listening to calming music).

- [ ] Prepared for Sleep: Basic hygiene (brushed teeth, washed face).

Phase 3: Sleep Environment Optimization

- [ ] Cool: Room temperature is cool (around 65°F/18°C).
- [ ] Dark: Room is completely dark (blackout curtains, eye mask).
- [ ] Quiet: Room is quiet (earplugs, white noise machine).
- [ ] Comfortable: Bedding and sleepwear are comfortable.

Consistency Check:

- [ ] Did I start my evening routine at a consistent time?
- [ ] Did I resist the urge to engage in Revenge Bedtime Procrastination?

Appendix B: The Night Owl's Toolkit

These tools can help you optimize your environment, manage your energy, and support your natural rhythm.

Sleep Environment Optimization

- **Blackout Curtains:** Essential for blocking out external light, especially in the summer months or if you live in an urban area.
- **Eye Mask:** A comfortable eye mask can help block out light if blackout curtains are not feasible, or when traveling.
- **White Noise Machine:** Helps mask disruptive sounds and create a consistent auditory environment.
- **Earplugs:** Essential for blocking out noise if you have a noisy environment or a partner with a different schedule.
- **Smart Lighting:** Smart bulbs can be programmed to dim in the evening and brighten in the morning.

Wake-Up Optimization

- **Wake-Up Light (Sunrise Alarm Clock):** Simulates a sunrise, gradually brightening your room to help you wake up gently and reduce sleep inertia. (Highly recommended for night owls).
- **Vibration Alarm:** A vibrating alarm (often found on smartwatches or specialized devices) can wake you up without disturbing your partner.
- **Light Therapy Lamp (10,000 lux):** Essential for getting bright light exposure in the morning, especially in the winter months or if you wake up before the sun. Helps regulate your circadian rhythm and boost alertness.

Productivity and Focus

- **Noise-Canceling Headphones:** Essential for protecting your peak hours and minimizing distractions, especially in open offices or busy households.

- **Productivity Apps (Use Sparingly):**
    - *To-Do Lists:* Use a simple app (e.g., Todoist, TickTick, or a physical notebook) to manage your priorities.
    - *Focus Timers:* Use the Pomodoro Technique or similar methods to structure your work sessions.
    - *Website Blockers:* Use apps (e.g., Freedom, Cold Turkey) to block distracting websites and apps during your peak hours.
- **Blue Light Filters/Glasses:** Use blue light filters on your screens (e.g., f.lux) or wear blue light blocking glasses in the evening to minimize the impact of blue light on your melatonin production.

Energy Management

- **Water Bottle:** Keep a large water bottle with you throughout the day to ensure adequate hydration.
- **Healthy Snacks:** Keep healthy snacks (protein, healthy fats) on hand to stabilize your energy levels.

Appendix C: Summary of Key Chronotype Research

This summary provides a brief overview of the scientific research supporting the concepts discussed in this book. This information can be useful for understanding your biology and communicating your needs to others.

1. Chronotypes are Real and Biological

- **Definition:** Chronotype is the individual difference in the timing of sleep and activity patterns, determined by the internal biological clock (circadian rhythm).
- **The Spectrum:** People fall on a spectrum from extreme morning types (Larks) to extreme evening types (Owls), with the majority falling in the middle (Hummingbirds).
- **Prevalence:** Approximately 40-60% of the population leans toward eveningness.

2. Genetics Play a Major Role

- **Clock Genes:** Research has identified specific genes, often called "clock genes," that regulate the circadian rhythm and influence chronotype.
- **Heritability:** Chronotype is highly heritable, meaning it is largely determined by genetics, not choice or willpower.

3. Hormonal Differences

- **Melatonin:** The timing of melatonin secretion (the sleep hormone) varies significantly between chronotypes. In Owls, melatonin is released later in the evening and persists later in the morning.
- **Cortisol:** The timing of cortisol awakening response (the stress hormone that boosts alertness) is also delayed in Owls.

4. Sleep Inertia and Cognitive Performance

- **Sleep Inertia:** The transitional state between sleep and wakefulness, characterized by impaired cognitive performance and grogginess.
- **Impact on Owls:** Sleep inertia is more severe and lasts longer in night owls, especially when they are forced to wake up early.
- **Peak Performance:** Cognitive performance peaks at different times for different chronotypes. Larks peak in the morning; Owls peak in the afternoon/evening.

5. Social Jetlag and Health Consequences

- **Definition:** Social jetlag is the misalignment between the biological clock and the social clock (work/school schedules).
- **Impact:** Chronic social jetlag is associated with increased risk of obesity, diabetes, cardiovascular disease, depression, and anxiety.

6. The Night Owl Advantage

- **Creativity:** Evening types tend to exhibit higher levels of creativity and divergent thinking.
- **Cognitive Strengths:** Night owls often perform well on tasks requiring inductive reasoning and analytical thinking.
- **Sustained Attention:** Night owls can maintain focus and attention for longer periods later in the day.

Conclusion

The scientific evidence clearly indicates that the traditional 9-to-5 schedule is detrimental to the health and productivity of a large portion of the population. Recognizing and respecting individual differences in chronotype is essential for creating a healthier, more equitable, and more productive society.

References

Archer, S. N., Robilliard, D. L., Skene, D. J., et al. (2003). A length polymorphism in the circadian clock gene Per3 is linked to delayed sleep phase syndrome and extreme diurnal preference. Sleep, 26(4), 413-419.

Barnes, C. M., & Wagner, D. T. (2009). Changing to an Early-Morning Start Time: The Influence of Chronotype and Sleep on Affect and Job Satisfaction. Journal of Applied Psychology, 94(5), 1319–1327.

Czeisler, C. A. (2015). Perspective: Casting light on sleep deficiency. Nature, 526(7575), S118.

Daghlas, I., Lane, J. M., Saxena, R., & Vetter, C. (2021). Genetically proxied diurnal preference, sleep timing, and risk of major depressive disorder. JAMA Psychiatry, 78(8), 903-910.

Dijk, D. J., & Czeisler, C. A. (1995). Contribution of the circadian pacemaker and the sleep homeostat to sleep propensity... The Journal of Neuroscience, 15(5 Pt 1), 3526–3538.

Dunster, G. P., de la Iglesia, L., Ben-Hamo, M., et al. (2018). Sleepmore in Seattle: Later school start times are associated with more sleep and better performance in high school students. Science Advances, 4(12), eaau6200.

Foster, R. G., Peirson, S. N., Wulff, K., et al. (2013). Sleep and circadian rhythm disruption in modern society. Nature Reviews Neuroscience, 14(8), 567-578.

Giampietro, M., & Cavallera, G. M. (2007). Morning and evening types and creative thinking. Personality and Individual Differences, 42(3), 453-463.

Hafner, M., Stepanek, M., Taylor, J., et al. (2017). Why sleep matters—the economic costs of insufficient sleep: A cross-country comparative analysis. Rand Health Quarterly, 6(4), 11.

Hilditch, C. J., & McHill, A. W. (2019). Sleep inertia: current insights. Nature and Science of Sleep, 11, 135-145.

Jones, S. E., Lane, J. M., Wood, A. R., et al. (2019). Genome-wide association study identifies 351 loci for chronotype in the UK Biobank... Nature Communications, 10(1), 2603.

Juda, M., Vetter, C., & Roenneberg, T. (2013). Chronotype modulates sleep duration, sleep quality, and social jet lag in shift-workers. Journal of Biological Rhythms, 28(2), 141–151.

Kelley, P., Lockley, S. W., Foster, R. G., & Wulff, K. (2015). Synchronizing education to adolescent biology: 'let teens sleep, start school later'. Learning, Media and Technology, 40(2), 210-226.

Knutson, K. L., & von Schantz, M. (2018). Associations between chronotype, morbidity and mortality in the UK Biobank cohort. Chronobiology International, 35(8), 1045–1053.

Kühnel, J., Bledow, R., & Feuerhahn, N. (2017). When do you flourish? A chronotype-fit perspective on work engagement and burnout. Journal of Organizational Behavior, 38(8), 1189-1205.

Patke, A., Murphy, P. J., Onat, O. E., et al. (2017). Mutation of the Human Circadian Clock Gene CRY1 in Familial Delayed Sleep Phase Disorder. Cell, 169(2), 203–215.e13.

Roberts, R. D., & Kyllonen, P. C. (1999). Morningness-eveningness and intelligence: Early to bed, early to rise will likely make you anything but wise!. Personality and Individual Differences, 27(6), 1123-1133.

Roenneberg, T., Wirz-Justice, A., & Merrow, M. (2003). Life between clocks: daily temporal patterns of human chronotypes. Journal of Biological Rhythms, 18(1), 80–90.

Roenneberg, T., Allebrandt, K. V., Merrow, M., & Vetter, C. (2012). Social Jetlag and Obesity. Current Biology, 22(10), 939–943.

Roenneberg, T., & Merrow, M. (2016). The circadian clock and human health. Current Biology, 26(10), R432-R443.

Roenneberg, T., Pilz, L. K., Zerbini, G., & Winnebeck, E. C. (2019). Chronotype and Social Jetlag: A (Self-) Critical Review. Biology, 8(3), 54.

Scheer, F. A. J. L., Hilton, M. F., Mantzoros, C. S., & Shea, S. A. (2009). Adverse metabolic and cardiovascular consequences of circadian misalignment. PNAS, 106(11), 4453–4458.

Scheer, F. A. J. L., Shea, T. J., Hilton, M. F., & Shea, S. A. (2008). An endogenous circadian rhythm in sleep inertia results in greatest cognitive impairment upon awakening during the biological night. Journal of Biological Rhythms, 23(4), 353–361.

Schmidt, C., Collette, F., Cajochen, C., & Peigneux, P. (2007). A time to think: circadian rhythms in human cognition. Cognitive Neuropsychology, 24(7), 755-789.

Vetter, C., Fischer, D., Matera, J. L., & Roenneberg, T. (2015). Aligning Work and Circadian Time in Shift Workers Improves Sleep and Reduces Circadian Disruption. Current Biology, 25(7), 907–911.

Wieth, M. B., & Zacks, R. T. (2011). Time of day effects on problem solving: When the non-optimal is optimal. Thinking & Reasoning, 17(4), 387-401.

Wittmann, M., Dinich, J., Merrow, M., & Roenneberg, T. (2006). Social Jetlag: Misalignment of Biological and Social Time. Chronobiology International, 23(1-2), 497–509.

Wong, P. M., Hasler, B. P., Kamarck, T. W., et al. (2015). Social Jetlag, Chronotype, and Cardiometabolic Risk. The Journal of Clinical Endocrinology and Metabolism, 100(12), 4612–4620.

www.ingramcontent.com/pod-product-compliance
Lightning Source LLC
LaVergne TN
LVHW021514080426
835509LV00018B/2512